The Funding Game

Rules for Public Library Advocacy

Mary Anne Craft

The Scarecrow Press, Inc.
Lanham, Maryland, and London
and
Neal-Schuman Publishers, Inc.
New York
1999

SCARECROW PRESS, INC.

Published in the United States of America
by Scarecrow Press, Inc.
4720 Boston Way
Lanham, Maryland 20706
http://www.scarecrowpress.com

4 Pleydell Gardens, Folkestone
Kent CT20 2DN, England

British Library Cataloguing in Publication Information Available

Library of Congress Cataloging-in-Publication Data

Craft, Mary Anne, 1939–
      The funding game : rules for public library advocacy / Mary Anne Craft.
         p.   cm.
      Includes bibliographical references and index.
      ISBN 0-8108-3593-2 (alk. paper)
      1. Public libraries—United States—Finance.   2. Fund raising—United
   States.   3. Public libraries—Public relations—United States.   I. Title.
   Z683.2.U6C73   1999   99-22572
   027.4'0973—dc21   CIP

∞ ™The paper used in this publication meets the minimum requirements of
American National Standard for Information Sciences—Permanence of
Paper for Printed Library Materials, ANSI/NISO Z39.48–1992.
Manufactured in the United States of America.

Contents

Rule 6. *Create and Innovate*

Rule 7. *Recap*

Rule 8. *In Conclusion*

Appendixes

Acknowledgments

I would like to thank the individuals mentioned in this book for their generous time and assistance in the research, and also the staff of the New York Public Library, the Carnegie Library of Pittsburgh, and the Library of the School of Library and Information Sciences at the University of Pittsburgh for the considerable help they gave me.

Preface

Game—a set of rules completely specifying a competition, including the permissible actions of and information available to each participant, the probabilities with which chance events may occur, the criteria for termination of the competition, and the distribution of payoffs.

—*The Heritage Illustrated Dictionary of the English Language*

The case is still at issue, but the initiative is the library's. The ball is in the library's court.

—M. A. Craft, "Private Funds versus Public Funds—the Ball Is in the Library's Court," *The Bottom Line,* vol. 8, no. 4 (1995), p. 9

This is a book about the funding game, or maximizing local dollars and funding potential for public libraries. The game is played to keep libraries growing, thriving, and performing as viable and essential community players. The method of play is library advocacy, which, as used here, is a library initiative that stimulates present or future funding from local public or private sources. When funding is the name of the game, all library initiatives by administrators, board members, staff, and Friends, whether inside or outside the library, are a form of advocacy because the library, as a public institution, is always on view and always accountable.

Most U.S. public libraries receive, on average, 78 percent or more of their funds from a local entity (city, county, or special tax district) and over 8 percent, in part, from gifts and donations.[1] Therefore, the relationship between the library and its funders is geographically close. The people who fund the library are the ones who use it or are related to the ones who use it or like to say they are.

The funding game is not an easy play. Little formal training is available where one would expect it, the coach is usually a novice, the players might be recruited against their will, and the opposition might keep a low profile until the last of the game, when they grab the take. All of this can make game strategy precarious.

However, one thing is clear: the scoreboard. When someone in charge wakes up one day (after years of rewarding engagement in pursuits learned in library school), glances at the scoreboard, and spots a firm, resolute zero, they instinctively know to get out the bat and glove, rev up the fans, ignite the fireworks, and throw themselves to the mercy of the funding game.

The funding game is getting dollars for a library, given mutually understood rules or initiatives governing the conduct between players; information obtained through research or intuition or by hook or crook; the probabilities of chance events, such as a major gift or budget initiative dropping in one's lap (in which case the game might be happily terminated); and an agreed-on distribution of winnings.

One caveat. Winning in the funding game does not mean winning "just any" funds. Rather, the dollars to be won must be *commensurate with a library's relative value as perceived by potential funders*. This is where the fans (a.k.a. library advocates) come in. Their job is to interpret the library to the community and the elected officials so that its position relative to other public funding needs is high on the priority list.

How do advocates do this? The answer is not on the reference shelf, in the latest CD-ROM, or on the computer screen. The answer lies in *relationships* with a capital "R," and these are relationships of all kinds—with the community, with partners, with teams, and in one-on-one encounters. Relationships either make it all happen or are blamed for its not happening. Any library director worth her (or his) team uniform is rarely in her office because she is out relating. (Book researchers, in particular, know this.) Or, if she is in her office, she is relating in person, on the telephone, or on the listserv. This method might be called "stirring." "I like to be out stirring around," said one public library director.

Library relationships that benefit present or future funding happen with just about every conceivable entity—staff, trustees, Friends, city council, the mayor, chief executive officers, business owners, nonprofit executives, voters, the media, members of community boards, union representatives, the poor, the housebound, the rich, gays, lesbians, the venerable opposition, the local mail carrier, and one's seatmate on the bus. They are all called into play on one team or another by the dedicated library advocate—be it administrator, trustee, Friend, or library user—who has committed him- or herself to keeping the team, the fans, the visitors, the playing field, and the game intact. Building these relationships is critical to success in the funding game.

Notes

1. National Center for Education Statistics, *Public Libraries in the U.S.* (Washington, D.C.: Bureau of the Census, 1995), p. iii.

Introduction

> Advocacy — active support; as of a cause; advocate — to speak in favor of, recommend; a person who argues for a cause; supporter or defender.
>
> —*The Heritage Illustrated Dictionary of the English Language*

The emphasis of this book is on local public library funding, which makes up the bulk of public library budgets. The discussion assumes a definition of public library advocacy to include library initiatives that facilitate present or future library funding, whether originated for that purpose (e.g., lobbying, referenda campaigns, and funding partnerships) or utilized in that context (e.g., library literacy and children's programs, outstanding public service, and public Internet access). Funds might be acquired in a relatively short time as a result of lobbying, grants, or other funding initiatives, or they might be facilitated over a longer period, as in long-term outreach efforts, partnerships, and community board participation that help build local funding support. Funds might also be a by-product of another effort, as in the leveraging that can occur following a donation of major funds.

The advocacy described in the following chapters includes both external and internal library efforts. External efforts — such as one-on-one relations with voters and funding officials, staff memberships in community organizations, solicitation of community input, and encouraging media coverage and otherwise keeping the public informed — are supported by internal efforts, such as attention to the planning and presentation of public services; involvement of library trustees, support staff, and Friends; and leveraging funds already in hand.

Library advocacy is a people-relationship initiative. It is a tri-partnership with the community and with voters or their elected representatives. Advocacy is a political process in the classic sense of "political," meaning relationships between people, as well as in the more common sense of lobbying government officials. As relationships are always in flux, depending on who is involved and for how long and when and where the relationship takes place and for what purposes, advocacy differs from one case to the next in terms of style and method. The advocacy that builds a partnership with the local Rotary Club over a long time might be called "softball advocacy," whereas the effort to obtain immediate funds from the city council to keep branch libraries open might be called "hardball advocacy."

Advocacy differs from one instance to the next with respect to techniques, timing, concentration of efforts, mobilizing of teams, and expectation of results. Hardball advocacy relies largely on hard copy, such as voter signatures, library user statistics, and social or economic data, when available. It springs into action immediately, employs all its resources simultaneously, and expects immediate results for the short haul. The Prince George's County Memorial Library's response to the threat of a $2 million budget cut is an example of hardball advocacy.

Softball advocacy, on the other hand, employs low-key techniques, such as community networking, public relations, and anecdotal stockpiling to persuade funders; works behind the scenes over a long time period (perhaps several years); uses its support system, such as Friends groups, for regularly planned activities (e.g., annual fund drives and special events); and gets the anticipated results in due course. The Rochester Hills Public Library's community partnerships, networking, and annual fund drives are examples of softball advocacy. Both hardball and softball advocacy might have their place at different times and for different players in the funding game, and hybrid forms—a little softball, a little hardball—work as well.

With the funding spotlight on it, the library takes on new forms, new thinking, and new practices and turns some of the old forms, thinking, and practices to funding advantage. Examples of these are presented in this book in field accounts, which consist of detailed descriptions of recent advocacy activities in public libraries selected by convenient sampling. The intention is to fairly represent current practices in library advocacy for funding advantage. The field accounts are not necessarily intended to illustrate exemplary solutions, although the activities of some libraries could certainly qualify in a lineup of superlative advocacy efforts. Rather, a goal of this book is that by presenting examples of library advocacy and citing a variety of community input, library administrators, board members, and Friends will have better insight into possibilities for their own library's funding advantage. They might pursue a dialogue with those who have been active in a particular arena as names and places are provided, or they might find new ways of thinking about what they already know, also spurring initiatives.

Another of the book's intentions is to emphasize the relation between various library activities and library funding so that they are better able to work for each other. Although this can result in what might be considered a lopsided assessment of public library activities, this is "the funding game," in which local stakes, which individual public libraries are going for, are high.

In the following chapters, discussion is organized by the following "rules of advocacy," which govern public library initiatives and have implications for library funding.

ThinkChange   Field accounts describing the funding implications of major recent changes in libraries—in stakeholders, facilities, technology, culture, and system organization.

Mobilize the Team   Field accounts of team efforts in soliciting private and public funds, cutting costs, and long-range planning with implications for funding.

Partner with Clout   Field accounts of partnerships that benefit funding through political, community, and business relationships.

Talk Assets   Field accounts of library initiatives in business, fine art, education, and youth and senior services that facilitate funding or funding advantage.

Mind the Opposition   The nature of library opposition from voters and public funders and the responses of public libraries.

Create and Innovate   Creative and innovative efforts on the part of public libraries that influence their funding.

Recap   An evaluation model for application to library advocacy efforts and a proposed library advocates' code of ethics.

What does it take to fund a library? What does it take to win a game? It takes new strategies, teamwork, partnering, leveraging assets, scoring in the face of opposition, creating, innovating, and, finally, reviewing all of this for the next round.

The details are presented in the following field accounts and discussions of current library practices. These are based on the author's personal interviews of principal players involved and her experience in the field. Quotations that are not footnoted are from personal interviews, faxes, or e-mail to the author.

Note: Budget figures are from, in order, the Public Library Data Service (PLDS), *Statistical Report* (Chicago: American Library Association, 1997), the *American Library Directory, 1997–98* (50th ed.), or directly from the library in question, when available. Dictionary definitions are from *The Heritage Illustrated Dictionary of the English Language, International Edition* (Boston: Houghton Mifflin, 1979).

RULE 1

THINKCHANGE (OR CHANGETHINK)

Chapter 1

Introduction

> Rapid change means chance. It means uncertainty. It means competition from the least-expected quarter. It means big projects that collapse and small ones that stun one with their success. It means new technologies, new kinds of skills and workers, and wholly unprecedented economic conditions.
>
> —Alvin Toffler, *Powershift*
> (New York: Bantam Books, 1990), p. 152

> It's a changing time . . . [it's] a game of changes. And there will be a lot of changes in this organization for the first time in quite some time.
>
> —Cam Bonifay, general manager of the Pittsburgh Pirates
> baseball team, in Paul Meyer, "Team's New Era Begins Today,"
> *Pittsburgh Post-Gazette,* September 29, 1996, p. D6

Funding is the name of the game, the library is the lead player, and ThinkChange—a library initiative for an alternative course of action—is a major stroke in library advocacy. The presence or absence of funds determines whether library programs, staffing, and hours of operation will continue (or even come about in the first place), and it is the library's initiatives that can determine the presence or absence of funds. Therefore, it is not surprising that library administrators are increasingly learning to speak the language of funding initiatives known as library advocacy.

This chapter discusses some of the ways in which ThinkChange influences public library funding:

- It brings in new stakeholders as funding partners.
- It builds new library buildings that generate new funding patterns.

- It prepares library culture to respond to funding crises.
- It adapts new technology that can facilitate the local economy.
- It consolidates resources to stimulate public funding.

Change affects funding, and funding brings about change. Change is the most obvious result of library funding issues—change in the availability of funds, change in the disbursement of funds, and change in the possibilities down the road. Other changes are in how libraries are managed, how they relate to the community, and how they think. Yet other changes take place in the culture of libraries. All these changes result from initiatives dictated largely by professional objectives and by initiatives with a stake in political agendas.

Before funds are available, ThinkChange lays the groundwork. Before bond issues finance new library buildings, before libraries recover budget deficits, and before they agree to funding for Internet access, ThinkChange sets the stage. Somewhere along the way, someone—library director, trustee, or Friend—has the wherewithal to ThinkChange for funding survival and to persuade others to come along.

ThinkChange is an initiative that has to take some material form—a new building, a new program, a new way of doing something—if it is to do any good.

Change is a tool that works on behalf of library funding, as are the other library initiatives discussed here: team building, partnerships, and promoting assets. However, more so than other tools, change is endowed with a special propensity to cause problems in its implementation, resulting in an assortment of stressful outcomes, some of which are touched on in the field reports.

Change has at least two implications for our discussion. First, it needs to be taken into consideration by the perpetrators of ThinkChange before they proceed too far, or the benefit to library funding can backfire, and everyone (including the library) loses. (See Scott and Jaffre, *Managing Change at Work,* in the bibliography.) Second, change emphasizes the fragile nature of the raw material of library advocacy—human relationships—and therefore calls for diligence on the part of advocates. Relationships have to be cultivated gradually to offset the downsides of change.

ThinkChange is partial to superlatives—bigger audiences, more stakeholders, broader purposes, wider access, larger space, new roles, and so on. More users, more reference questions, more materials circulating, more postcards on council members' desks, and more librarians on the Rotary board all feed the need for more dollars from local funders. When library budgets are cut, numbers seem to grow. Were funding shortages invented that libraries might expand their vision of themselves? Probably not, but they sure do help.

The field reports and comments in chapters 2 through 7 illustrate some of the effects of introducing change as well as what change does or could do in terms of funding a public library.

Chapter 2

New Stakeholders:
San Francisco Public Library

> People don't like too much change, but we know we have to change,
> and there will be great changes when we move to the new building.
>
> —Gil McNamee, former library employee and manager and
> current volunteer and guide, San Francisco Public Library,
> *San Francisco Examiner,* Fall 1995

> The question is, how do you mount tremendous change in an insti-
> tution without destroying the institution? Lots of people prefer not
> to change. We used to look to librarians to know what was best, but
> now we are dealing with the community mind. We need to change
> how the library operates.
>
> —Steven A. Coulter, president, San Francisco Public Library
> Commission, and vice president, Pacific Bell

Library income: $38.7 million
Local government share: 98 percent

On April 18, 1996, which was the ninetieth anniversary of the most famous San
Francisco earthquake, the "New Main" of the San Francisco Public Library
opened its doors to the public. This event, anticipated by the library Friends for
forty years,[1] was an "earthquake" not of disaster but of triumph for a library
system that only a few years before had cut budgets, reduced staff, and been
threatened by branch closings in a controversy with local government. To pay
the bills, a new generation of stakeholders was ushered in—foundations, corporations, and individuals—who set precedent in the library world both for
their enthusiastic response and for the questions raised by the onlookers in the

stands. The latter rebelled at what they considered an invasion of their turf from two quarters: the corporations whose logos were highlighted in the new building and the library foundation that raised the dollars to make it all possible.

The building had been financed by a 1988 bond measure, approved by a hefty 78 percent of the voters (California's infamous proposition 13 requires a two-thirds majority of voter approval for new tax measures), that designated $104.5 million for construction costs. So that the new building would have furnishings and interior appointments deserving of its handsome modernist design,[2] the San Francisco Public Library Foundation (already in existence for the capital campaign) took on the goal of raising $30 million. This goal, viewed as outrageous to virtually all concerned, including those charged with its fulfillment, was achieved, and even surpassed, well in advance of the building's opening. Considering that no history of library fund-raising existed on which to draw and that the city was already immersed in capital campaigns for three important art institutions, the result was a major coup. Figuring largely in the project's success was the novel idea of "affinity groups"—in-depth collections supported by specialized community interests—which contributed to a third of the funding goal (see chapter 6).

Enthusiasm for the funding campaign seemed to be especially strong among the city's foundations. Commenting on the lineup of contributors, Steven A. Coulter, president of the library commission and vice president of Pacific Bell, noted that community foundations contributed more than had been expected, whereas major individual donors kept to their traditional patterns of local giving that favored the other capital campaigns; similarly, less than the expected contributions came from the city's major corporations.

The San Francisco Foundation, a forty-year-old community foundation, provided a novel approach by using an especially liberal interpretation of the library's audience and then piecing together funds from a number of portfolios in its stewardship. It felt justified in going to extraordinary lengths because its mandate is to serve the disadvantaged and because it felt that the campaign would be a difficult one "in that the majority of potential donors are not users of the public library system."[3] Assembling funds from an arts and humanities endowment, an educational trust for minority programs, and four trusts for the disabled, the foundation donated a total of $875,000—the largest award it had ever made to a cultural organization.

Another community foundation, the William G. Gilmore Foundation, pledged $100,000, citing in a written statement by its president, Robert C. Harris, "Our trustees urge me to emphasize that they all consider the new library and the campaign the Library Foundation is conducting, one of, and perhaps the, most important project for our City. In our view, nothing can take the place of a centrally located modern library with such fine plans especially for children's education."[4]

Major corporate support came from three corporations: BankAmerica, which funded the library's Jobs and Career Center; Pacific Bell; and Chevron, which funded the Chevron Teen Center, in part because "our chairman was a manager of the campaign," said a program officer for Chevron. Each corporation contributed $200,000 or more.

With the added help of prominent local philanthropists and community leaders, the library's foundation raised a total of $34 million from 17,000 donors of wide-ranging interests, satisfying a campaign criterion of "one whose doors were open to everyone."[5] According to a foundation program officer, "There was a lot of enthusiasm for giving because it was a chance to benefit the entire community, not just the more affluent who donate to the opera and other cultural organizations."

The following examples from the local media indicate the enthusiasm with which the New Main was received:

> The most advanced public library in the nation opens in San Francisco in just ten days, and make no mistake. You don't have to be computer-literate; you don't have to speak English; heck, you don't even have to know how to read to enjoy and benefit from hundreds of state-of-the art resources at the incredible building we now call the new Main San Francisco Public Library in Civic Center.[6]
>
> The general Bay Area media has gone ga-ga over the new Main. Every major paper and television station has done something, or many something's on it. San Francisco has seen a lot of bad projects lately. This is hailed as something that actually worked.[7]

However, library staff opposed the place of corporate interests in a free public library and the possible influence that the library's foundation as a private entity might have on public library policy. These appeared as follows in the city's news media and elsewhere:

> Some of the centers and rooms bear not merely family names, but are named for consumer goods like Chevron, and thus constitute not merely a thank you but are a form of advertising. Another problematic aspect at SFPL is that some of these corporate donors are not merely listed on a plaque off to the side, but are permanently and deeply etched in glass over the reference desk, as in Chevron Teen Center.[8]
>
> The Chevron Teen Center targets a youth market just on the brink of buying gasoline and oil for first cars. The Hormel Gay and Lesbian Center sanctions a meat-processing giant that gained notoriety as a union-buster in the mid-'80s. [The Hormel Center is, in fact, named for James C. Hormel, San Francisco philanthropist and community leader, not for the foods giant.] "Pacific Bell" are the first words a child sees when looking up at the street banners that advertise the new Main. There's an Alice in Wonderland thing dubbed the Bank of America Jobs and Careers Center. An affinity group? Didn't Bank of America cut short the jobs and careers of its work force through layoff just a few years ago? . . . If Pacific Bell is a heavy contributor, will the library spend more on modems and less on print materials?[9]
>
> The big problem was that the foundation and the library administration worked out this agreement and the staff was not involved. We were shocked and dismayed

that this private organization [the library foundation]—with no membership and no public accountability or open-meeting policy—was being given so much power. This is a public library and the whole concept of free and equal access is in jeopardy.[10]

Library policymakers defended their position:

If the foundation was a public entity, frankly, we would not have made any money. If you did not have confidentiality of records, I can tell you that no donor would be giving anything. I know that because donors told me [so] . . . at the very beginning of this process.[11]

People don't give money to an institution and say, "Do whatever you want to with it," except in very few cases. . . . They've given us money for furnishings and services, but it comes with strings attached.[12]

Commenting on the controversy, a foundation representative said, "In a city where you have very vocal groups seeking a political platform for recognition, to involve the community as a means of getting broad support could clear the air on issues such as, 'Is it realistic to expect a business to give and not receive public recognition?'" A suggestion proposed by this individual was to have community meetings in various neighborhoods early on in the process to solicit public input.

Speaking to the question of gaining support of the library staff for the new corporate stakeholders, Sherry Thomas, executive director of the San Francisco Public Library Foundation, said, "Looking back, we should have done training workshops for staff to prepare them for fundraising—tell them what it would mean to their organization and find out how they feel about it. The line staff were shocked at the corporate-named rooms, they thought they should have been consulted. We at the foundation didn't know they weren't informed. The practice of providing naming opportunities is commonplace in the fundraising world."

In Thomas's opinion, "Libraries need a cultural shift. With diminishing public resources, fundraising is going to become a fact of life in the next quarter century."

Comment

From this example, library advocates can learn that, despite odds that could be insurmountable for another organization (i.e., no funding base from which to work, other major campaigns running at the same time, potential major donors holding to their former giving habits, and so on), the library succeeded and even overran its goal—a goal apparently chosen somewhat on impulse without the prior agreement of those who were running the campaign and one that was considered far too optimistic. Why did it succeed? Back to the axiom "The public loves libraries." Funds add up because much of the public, representative of many sectors, is willing to donate. Advocates need to hammer away at funding efforts and set goals higher.

Regarding the issue of the best time to have a campaign, library advocates in other areas of the country have documented that there is no "right time" for a campaign, although campaign advisers might try to convince the library to wait if other campaigns are being conducted. The library's wait might be to the advantage of the other campaigns but not necessarily to the library's. Advice to advocates from the experts is to jump in and get your feet wet: "the public loves libraries."

The glowing media reports reflect especially the groundswell of community support that the new building had and that is advisable for advocates to encourage, so that the impact of the new building will have reverberations lasting through as many fiscal years as possible.

The opposition provides an illustration of what can happen when change is ill managed. The impact of the project calling into play so many donors and assorted others with their own particular needs and hopes could hardly be expected to proceed without some heckling from the stands—in this city's yeasty culture. However, the opposition in this case reached an unusually strong crescendo that was heard in many corners of the library world and the world at large (partly because of the Internet's listservs) until finally the library director resigned.

The chief causes of the complaints—the concern that policy will be dictated by the new stakeholders threatening taxpayers' rights and the library's mission of unbiased service—were those that, at least from the safety seat of retrospect, would seem to lend themselves to treatment by proven techniques of managing change, including training workshops referred to by the foundation director. Library administration might have anticipated the extent of negative reaction if they had early on encouraged interactive communications with library staff, as library advocates are learning to do in the community. They might also have looked to the community to determine how change affects other organizations locally; this has implications for the library as well. A rule of advocacy is to be aware of what is happening elsewhere in the community. Taking these steps could well have averted some of the problems associated with change without running the risk of injuring the library's image and future funding.

Notes

1. Sam Whiting, "A Friend for Life, Marjorie Stern," *San Francisco Chronicle Special Report,* "Library of the Future," April 7, 1996, p. 35.
2. The building was designed by eminent architect James Ingo Freed, designer of

the U.S. Holocaust Memorial Museum in Washington, D.C., and a partner in Pei Cobb Freed & Partners, New York. Freed was a German immigrant who learned to read English at the Chicago Public Library. See Jesse Hamlin, "Shedding Light on the Subject," *San Francisco Chronicle Datebook,* April 7, 1996, p. 33.

3. San Francisco Public Library Foundation, *The New Main* (summer 1991), p. 9.

4. San Francisco Public Library Foundation, *The New Main* (summer 1991), p. 8.

5. Anne Lowrey Bailey, "How a New Idea Saved the San Francisco Library's Stalled Capital Campaign," *The Chronicle of Philanthropy,* July 12, 1994, p. 27.

6. Patricia Holt, "The New Main Lights the Way," book review, *San Francisco Chronicle,* April 7, 1996, p. 1.

7. Pub-Adv listserv, April 24, 1996.

8. San Francisco Public Library staff member, Pub-Adv listserv, April 24, 1996.

9. San Francisco Public Library children's librarian, "Corporations Invade S.F.'s New Main Library and Branches," *San Francisco Examiner,* June 12, 1996, p. A17.

10. Chief steward of the Librarian's Guild and manager at the Presidio Branch, San Francisco Public Library, in Nina Siegal, "Library for Sale," *San Francisco Bay Guardian,* April 17, 1996, quoted on Pub-Adv listserv, April 19, 1996.

11. Steven A. Coulter, in Siegal, "Library for Sale."

12. Dale Carlson, former library commissioner, San Francisco Public Library, in Siegal, "Library for Sale."

Chapter 3

New Central Buildings: Chicago Public Library and Oxnard Public Library, Oxnard, California

> For sheer heft, roominess and promised ease of use, Chicago at last has the central public library it has wanted for most of the century.
>
> —M. W. Newman, "Here's One Magnificent Library,"
> *Chicago Sun Times,* September 29, 1991, special section, p. 2

> "The new public library—the county's largest—reinstates Oxnard's role as the major provider of library services in this county," boasted City Manager Vernon Hazen. "The rest of the county needs to look up to us in that regard."
>
> —Howard Breuer, "Kids Give Thumbs up to Library,"
> *Star Free Press* (Ventura County, Calif.), March 8, 1992
> (photocopy from Oxnard Public Library)

Library incomes: Chicago, $71.1 million; Oxnard, $2.3 million
Local government shares: Chicago, 85 percent; Oxnard, 96 percent

Neither the size of an urban metropolis nor the geography of a Pacific coast beach community seem to dampen public enthusiasm for new library buildings. The question is, Is funding benefited? The experience of the Harold Washington Library Center of the Chicago Public Library would indicate, at this point in time, that it is, whereas at the Oxnard Public Library, which opened at about the same time, the question is still at large.

Whether building new main facilities is to be commended or condemned has been a lively question in library circles, fueled by gadfly Charles W. "Give 'em

What They Want" Robinson, retired director of the Baltimore County Public Library in Towson, Maryland. In 1992, Robinson and his staff wrote,

> We continue to build massive, expensive central libraries in the downtown of core cities, like the recently erected, highly expensive, glowering Bastille-like Harold Washington Library in Chicago. Just before the opening of this library—which received glowing accolades from the library press—it was announced by the City of Chicago that over 100 staff members would be cut from the library's budget. . . . But any modern retailer, any thinking librarian interested in the client-centered service, would and can recognize this building as a financial service and administrative disaster. . . . The folly is being duplicated in large cities across the country. . . . Few leaders in the library profession have spoken out, on the record, about this massive waste of library resources, resources, which, if spent on materials and services that the people we serve want and need, might increase the actual use and relevancy of public libraries in these cities.[1]

On the other hand, a new building can have "an extremely positive effect on the entire library system," according to Commissioner Mary A. Dempsey of the Chicago Public Library (serving 2,784,000). Dempsey came on the scene two years after the library's ten-story, 730,000-square-foot Harold Washington Library Center (HWLC) opened in October 1991 in Chicago's South Loop. Designed by the Sebus Group and its lead architect, Thomas H. Beeby, it replaced temporary quarters and an old central library building totaling 220,000 square feet of usable library space. Cited in the *Guinness Book of Records* as the largest public library building in the world,[2] the HWLC has enabled partnerships, promoted staff cooperation, and triggered new public and private funding. Favorably positioned to capitalize on burgeoning business and residential communities in downtown Chicago, the facility serves 6,000 persons daily and is open seven days a week. It was financed by a 1987 bond issue of $144 million.

Dempsey said that the Chicago Public Library Foundation, which raised an endowment of $12 million to $13 million annually for books, programs, and other materials, continues to do well and has added another of $10 million for systemwide automation in an effort dubbed "Project Mind."

The City of Chicago has also given "very healthy support," said Dempsey, citing, for example, a book budget increase from $8 million to $11 million from 1993 to 1996. According to a library news release in November 1996, "Since taking office in 1989, Mayor Richard M. Daley has been a strong proponent of public libraries, opening an unprecedented 31 new or renovated Chicago Public Library buildings." In 1996, the city approved the library's call for "more certainty in our funding, so we don't always have to vie with other city agencies," as Dempsey put it, by making a separate tax levy for operating funds. In addition, the library was awarded $50 million in capital funding for a three-year project of expansion and renovation. The latter was supported by a property tax increase equivalent to "$6 for an average size home or less than the cost of an average size paperback book," said Dempsey.

Having the HWLC had been "very beneficial" for several reasons that affect funding, according to Dempsey. Not only has it enabled more cost-efficient solutions to such agenda as library institute days for all staff—"from librarians to truck drivers"—so they could be held in one place and the transfer of certain technical services from a warehouse to the HWLC so that all technical processes could be housed under the same roof, but the library's "very visible presence" in the downtown cultural milieu has made it possible to "forge partnerships with local museums and the symphony," said Dempsey.

In addition, the HWLC generates $200,000 per year in room rental fees. The Winter Garden on the top floor of the building is a reading room by day and a banquet facility by night. Dempsey advised on the importance of providing for flexibility of space in planning new buildings, not only for library materials but also for community needs. Because of several spaces in the library that were not designated, the library was able to install a special collections reading room and, next to the Winter Garden, a restaurant that generates revenues for the library of at least $30,000 per year, as required in the contract with the outside concession that operates it.

Two thousand miles west, on the Pacific coast just north of Los Angeles, the new Oxnard Public Library opened in March 1992 in a gala ceremony attended by 500 well-wishers and letters of congratulations from First Lady Barbara Bush and California Governor Pete Wilson.[3] Although a city financial crisis loomed, a year earlier the library board had squelched attempts of the city council to appropriate part of the new space for city offices. In a strongly worded letter, the board wrote, "The building doesn't allow for just moving another department or division in without significant changes to the design. There would also be design fees for the architect, fees for blueprint revisions, change orders, an expensive halt to construction while these documents were assembled, and the cost of labor to tear out framing already built."[4]

Designed by the San Francisco firm Whisler-Patri Inc., the new $12.8 million, 72,000-square-foot library replaced a building one-quarter the size.[5] "The new building says that the city cares about the library and the people it serves," said Cathy R. Thomason, who, as one of a four-member library managing team, is also pioneering a new concept in library administration. Other signs of increased prosperity for the new library that serves 1,000 to 1,500 users daily throughout Ventura County are a doubling of membership in the library's Friends group from the start of construction to building opening and, in the four years following the library's opening, a 21 percent increase in circulation, to 533,000 annually.[6] There was also a budget increase of 30 percent, including building maintenance costs that went from $150,000 in the former facility to $277,000 in the new building. The new space allows for a fifteen-by-twenty-foot used-books and gift store, operated by the Friends, from which annual revenue, donated to the library or applied to special library projects, totals about $12,000.

Where the city financial crisis took its toll was in the city's portion of the library's budget, which slacked off 3 percent, according to Thomason, causing branch closings and reduced hours of opening in all library facilities, including the new central one. The risk factor in financing by municipal bonds, usually not a problem in the many U.S. public library capital projects that are funded this way (including the new San Francisco Main opened four years after Oxnard's), was a problem in this case because of a recession and a major drought.[7]

Financing was approved in 1988 in an $11 million bond issue to be repaid by capital growth fees charged to developers. A projected 350 new residential units were expected annually. This made sense in 1988, before the recession and the drought affected Ventura County in the 1990s, causing the growth rate to plummet.

Not unusual in the funding game, some questioned the building of the new library in the first place. For example, a local television service manager said that he was not convinced a newer, bigger library was even needed. "I never saw more that 30 people in the old library. I think Ventura [a neighboring city] spends their money a lot better than we do."[8] This observation contradicted media reports of overcrowding and a lack of space for 50,000 books in storage.[9]

Commenting on the library and its financing, City Manager Tom Frutchey was optimistic. Citing in particular the value of the library's preschool programs for a "poor" community, Frutchey said that growth needs to pay for the library. "Over a twenty- to twenty-five-year period, there will be cyclical ups and downs. We just happened to hit the down period at the beginning."

Financial crises notwithstanding, Oxnard will go down in the annals of library advocacy for the words of Councilwoman Dorothy Maron opposing the closing of a branch library. "Everybody needs a library," said Maron. "It's paramount to life."[10]

Comment

Good reasons exist for not constructing new library buildings, but if a library finds it necessary to play the funding game, certain pluses are inherent in a new building that can put the library in a winning position. As described previously, a new library (1) attracts the attention of public funders whose role of stakeholder is reinforced as they must weigh various issues in deciding how to fund the new building, (2) attracts the attention of the community (membership in Friends groups multiplies), and (3) introduces new funding mechanisms (e.g., private funding, additional public funding, and income from meeting rooms, restaurants, and gift stores) and partnerships because the library with a new facility is now a more attractive partner. With all the evidence, why not build a building on as grand a scale as possible to befit a grand city? Anything less would forfeit the library's share of the public spotlight to some other entity—a sports arena perhaps? If public library advocacy is to meet its objectives, it has to reflect the public mind-set—which, for better or worse, is the desire for new and bigger.

Oxnard played to the stands as a good advocate in a gala opening ceremony with politically correct invitees. Its Friends also know how to speak up in take-it-or-leave-it dealing with local politicians. However, the somewhat risky nature of its financing solution might be a warning to advocates. It might be that the library had such a strong constituency ("the public loves libraries") that emotion overwhelmed reason. Although some might have asked what the alternatives would be if the bottom were to fall out of the capital growth fees, the possibility was probably considered as remote as snow on the beach and, as the mayor would have us believe, not really of consequence in any case. Nevertheless, for reasons of community responsibility, it is advisable for advocates to give thought to the future of their funding proposals, as far as possible, so as not to jeopardize either the library's or other interests in the community.

It is to the advantage of both Chicago and Oxnard that probably nothing is more visible in library advocacy than a library building—the New York Public Library spotlighted its building to mark the library's centennial—and a new building is the most visible of all. How long this initiative can be played to advantage probably depends on a number of issues—political agendas for one. Both Chicago and Oxnard have the current advantage of local mayoral support. This kind of support is best nourished in projects and partnerships with a view to political expediencies: preschool reading, adult literacy, cost-savings initiatives, and a host of others that librarians and advocates discover are trump cards.

Notes

1. Baltimore County Public Library's Blue Ribbon Committee, *Give 'Em What They Want!* (Chicago: ALA, 1992).

2. Chicago Public Library, "Self-Guided Tour of the Harold Washington Library Center," brochure, May 1995.

3. Jim Schultz, "Library to Open Doors of Knowledge," *The Press-Courier* (Oxnard, Calif.), March 1992, Area News, p. 5.

4. Letter to the editor, *The Press-Courier* (Oxnard, Calif.), February 17, 1991, p. 5.

5. "Ceremony Set to Celebrate New Library," *Press Courier* (Ventura County, Calif.), June 27, 1990, p. 13.

6. Oxnard Public Library, "Selected Statistics, 1990–97," unpublished.

7. Howard Breuer, "Drought Chokes Oxnard's Need for Growth," *Star-Free Press* (Ventura County, Calif.), February 10, 1991, p. A3.

8. Breuer, "$1 Million a Year Needed to Repay $12.8 Million Bill," *Star-Free Press* (Ventura County, Calif.), March 2, 1992, p. 1.

9. Breuer, "$1 Million a Year Needed to Repay $12.8 Million Bill," p. 1.

10. Breuer, "Oxnard Center May Get Axed," *Star-Free Press* (Ventura County, Calif.), March 26, 1991, p. 1.

Chapter 4

Culture Shift:
Prince George's County Memorial
Library, Hyattsville, Maryland

> When major change hits a company, or a severe crisis demands a
> response, what really changes is the "corporate culture." The way
> the organization has been doing things. This much change demands
> a major shift in the way in which the work gets done. It is no longer
> possible to remain a caretaker, set in your ways.
>
> —Cynthia D. Scott and Dennis T. Jaffre, *Managing Change at
> Work,* rev. ed. (Menlo Park, Calif.: Crisp Publications, 1995), p. 12

Library income: $15.8 million
Local government share: 61 percent

When the Prince George's County Memorial Library (PGCML) in Hyattsville, Maryland, was threatened with a $2 million budget cut in 1996, it launched an initiative that restructured the culture of the library. According to library director William R. "au contraire" Gordon ("au contraire" was Gordon's response when informed of the possible cut), the teams were aggressively assembled: a business PAC of county businesses, independent Friends groups reorganized under one umbrella, and a 501(c)3 foundation established to pick up where the others left off. Retail stores and restaurants, women's clubs, local community foundations, and a core of volunteers also responded to the call.

How did the library manage, as Gordon put it, "all these people milling around on our behalf?" By appointing a development officer and "some resident schmoozers, the two most extroverted people we could find (one, a librarian)— the kind of people who stand on top of buildings and fling their business cards out." They became full-time public relations officers while the development office was charged with raising funds for library programs and their own offices.

ThinkChange became a priority for the entire staff. "It always stunned me what limited interest staff had in their libraries," said Gordon, who has spent thirty-five years in library service. Meeting with full staff once a year, touring branches twice a year, and meeting with branch librarians monthly, Gordon said that he manages "by wandering around and asking questions—do you realize what's going on, do you vote in your community, do you understand the bond issue? [In 1996, voters passed a library bond issue for $3 million in capital improvements.] I make a point to everybody that we are not keeping any secrets. Anything anyone wants to know, just ask."

Manager of the Oxon Hill branch, Evelyn Tchiyuka, said that she learned from the library administration "how important certain kinds of issues are in affecting how people perceive us." In monthly branch library meetings, Gordon reports on legislative issues and "expects us to go through it with our staff—all aspects from submission of budget to county committee," said Tchiyuka. "He asks us what questions we have so that when the public says, 'how come you have a budget problem? I thought you were part of the Board of Education,' we can answer knowledgeably." Previous to ThinkChange, only top administrative staff had this information from the budget hearings they attended. Afterward, all levels of staff became interested in what they could do "to get around begging every year," said Tchiyuka. "The staff isn't allowed to lobby [legal stipulation], but they can get the Friends groups to speak to concerns in ways we can't. The staff speaks up now in support of legislation for the library. We know we can't overturn Trim [the local tax-limiting initiative] legally, but we understand the idea of property tax revenue and we can make it known that if you really believe in the library in this county, you must help [the customers understand]."

"Advocacy is not something you do at the end of a day or week," said Gordon. "It becomes a significant part of your job." Outside of work, the staff talked to property owners "in ways we never thought of before, like 'we'll be looking at the same flat budget of $15.5 million if you don't go to bat for the library.' We never would have done that five years ago. Then we just gave the customer the information—the printed material we had at the reference desk [and kept quiet]," said Tchiyuka.

Because of the library's insistence on linking advocacy with outstanding public service, Gordon said that a trainer in customer relations was hired to train library staff—teaching them, among other things, "how to be polite." "The better you can do your job, the better you are at customer services," said Gordon. "If you want support, you must give good service. Don't take out your frustrations on the customers." Referring to a neighboring county that did not answer library phones on weekends, he said, "We're so devoted to customer service, we would never think of doing that."

To deal with the budget crisis of 1996, Friends groups of the county branches organized 300 demonstrators to present a petition of 71,000 names they had collected in a grassroots campaign to restore the library's $2 million budget cut, according to Barbara Simon, president of the Friends of the Prince George's County Libraries. (Among the persuasive arguments, said Gordon, was that "Spiro Agnew was from [neighboring] Baltimore County and he stole more than we're asking for.") "We wanted names," said Gordon. "We wanted to show elected officials that our business PAC was so powerful that if they didn't do what we asked, we might affect their reelection." The petition went directly to the governor of Maryland, and at midnight on the final day of debate, the last piece of state legislation gave the county its $2 million for the library.

The Friends and the library managed this extraordinary effort not just once but three times in successive years, for the 1996–98 fiscal year budgets. Can they continue? "People get tired of fighting battles," said Gordon. Community relations officer Natalie W. Weikart said, "How many times can you appeal to the state for a 'teacher's pet kind of allotment'? Why should the rest of the state help us out if we can't pay for our own services?" As the tax-capping legislation was not repealed by voters in a 1996 election, Weikart said, "Its retention is seen by other jurisdictions in Maryland as an indication that our county does not care about these services. . . . Until county residents are willing to shoulder some of this burden themselves, the library will probably continue to face severe budget problems."

The solution? More change, said Gordon. Change on the part of elected officials to see the legitimacy of a special tax district (not yet an alternative in the state) and change on the part of voters to repeal TRIM, the tax-limiting provision.

Meanwhile, the staff continues in a ThinkChange mode. For example, they adopted the term *customers* to replace *patrons*. "There hasn't been a lot of turnover in our staff, so it was hard to make the change from patrons when we'd been saying it for 25 years," said Tchiyuka. "It created a little stir at first— 'what's this deal about customers?' some would ask. However, the staff makes the connection that we are talking about an exchange of services as in the business world and a return on our product. In the mind of a staff member, there is a subliminal message. A customer demands certain products, and if we want repeated business, we must pay attention to our product quality. [In return], we expect loyalty on the part of the customer. We look at it like a business model— the customer is the priority."

Comment

This account is an example of hardball advocacy, mentioned in this book's introduction. The library responds to a crisis with every possible resource at hand and also invents new ones to leverage political influence and prevent a threatened budget cut. Hardball advocacy involves a broad interpretation of the library's constituency, calling them all into play, and strategies such as petition signing and dedicating one's efforts—near and far, in person or away—until the crisis is resolved and then taking action to head off the possibility of a repeat performance in the future.

On the home front, the library underwent a cultural change. Staff became knowledgeable about local funding issues, reviewed public service in a new light, learned to speak business-ese, kept the issue of funding in front of the public, and helped support Friends' efforts. The important link between advocacy and "outstanding public service" recurs several times in this book. The mention that weekend telephone hours will not be cut like the neighboring county's were is reflected in a current debate among library administrators as to whether to cut the obvious (library hours and branch closings) to emphasize the crisis to the public or to cut the least obvious, continuing to give priority to outstanding public service.

The library's task is to use its broad-based community support to develop new tactics to gather the support to implement a long-term funding solution— a difficult assignment for advocates given the current legal and political configurations.

Chapter 5

New Technology: Stanly County Public Library, Albemarle, North Carolina

> Asked to name the most exciting event ever to take place in Stanly County, Dotty Plyer, the Albemarle town historian, has a ready answer: the 1940 Little League World Series. "We beat a team from San Diego right here in Stanly County," she says. "That was by far the biggest thing that ever happened around here."
>
> —Greg Jaffe, "In a region of riches, county loses jobs, hope," *Wall Street Journal*, January 31, 1996, Southeast edition, p. S1

> We're very pleased we'll be working with Stanly County, our most rural neighbor, in the Rural Access part of our project. The Director and the staff at the Stanly County Library will be great participants. They are very enthusiastic about the project and see its potential for their community.
>
> —Pat Ryckman, Public Library of Charlotte and Mecklenburg County, from the Libraries Online! home page, December 1996

Library income: $737,000
Local government share: 85 percent

When the Stanly County Public Library, located in the rural Appalachian highlands of Albemarle, North Carolina, installed a public Internet system, the change was facilitated by a technically literate staff, an already existing online catalog, and grant dollars siphoned through the Public Library of Charlotte and Mecklenburg County (PLCMC). The grant, from Libraries Online![1] and the State Library of North Carolina, enabled PLCMC, some forty miles southeast of Stanly, to extend Internet access from its local network, Charlotte's Web, to neighboring rural libraries. The library received this initiative with great interest and an eye to its role in the county's economic development on the heels of the textile mill closings, most recently Fruit of the Loom's factory, which occupied ten downtown city blocks.[2]

Changes at the library following public Internet access have affected staff use of time, marketing the new product, and budget considerations. Library director Penny H. Welling said that staff are "very much busier working with people," that they stay busier, and that they use time differently; for example, they assist users more at the computer terminals than at the reference desk, they help job seekers interpret information retrieved on the Internet, they weigh the pros and cons of using the Internet as opposed to print sources, they keep statistics on equipment use as requested by Microsoft (the corporate funder of the new system in its Libraries Online! project), and they determine the effective use of volunteers (e.g., as class instructors in "how to" settings rather than posting them at computer terminals).

The way the budget is allocated for reference and information services has also changed. Welling said, "We expect to buy fewer print resources, especially expensive, seldom used materials, that contain information we can locate on the Internet, but we will have more telephone charges and greater staffing needs for computer support." The cost of additional phone usage was estimated at $200 per month, and print cartridge costs were to be added to the budget, as were staff time to manage the equipment and maintenance costs of $100 per hour.

The library staff has been "real savvy" about computers and the Internet, said Marianne Dalier, president of the Stanly County Chamber of Commerce. "They were some of the first in the state for a small community of our size to get their catalog online. This speaks well for our community in attracting new businesses, some of which are just now learning to use the Net." The library's access also helps link the county with its nearest urban center, Charlotte, to which a major highway is not yet available.

Commissioner Martha Sue Hall, who sits on the library's board of trustees, said that library services to the county population are so important that "we have got to continue to provide these" in an up-to-date format. She said that the library has set up a policy regarding the use of the Internet by children to prevent them from viewing "inappropriate material. This is a real stickler with me," said Hall, the mother of a ten-year-old. "I've done so much work with the courts, I know we have to protect our citizens."

For the staff of the Stanly County Library, the early results of change are mostly positive. They have participated in training workshops in Internet access to better serve library users, and they also enjoy using the Internet for their own personal benefit. One staff member was able to track down members of her father's fighting battalion in World War II for a planned reunion, and users have located information on "obscure diseases that a public library of this size would [otherwise] never be able to do," said Welling. In addition, in the local push to recruit new business, county department heads use the library's Internet access.

Marketing the Internet so that the community is aware of how to use it has also become a priority. First-year marketing costs were provided in the grant support. Consequently, the library held a "Grand Opening Day" for the community. It also places notices of noteworthy Web sites in newspaper announcements and provides instructive classes, such as the four sessions of "How to Get Your First Job," presented by the human resource officers of local companies, for teenagers fourteen years and older.

Although one of the stipulations of the computer installation was to set up a "fairly maintenance-free system," according to Welling, indications are that the super-hype tool is not maintenance free (nor is the staff!). "I love the Internet," said a library associate on staff, "but the frequency with which the system is down is causing us all 'technostress'. Also, the necessary time limitations imposed on the use of the library's four terminals—a one-hour limitation—has brought patrons nearly to blows with reference staff."

How has funding fared with the new technology in place? "It's been about level for the past few years," said Welling. According to Hall, "The legislature has their head in the right place about funding." They had just emerged from finalizing the county budget the previous day and had managed to keep it intact with no tax increase. The library budget might have had a few small cuts, said Hall, but "the things they really need are there."

Comment

Advocacy in the form of new services can play an especially significant role given a community's economic development priorities. As the county's resources in this example would have many demands placed on them, the fact that the library can provide Internet access for county offices, make it possible to advertise the area to businesses elsewhere seeking possible relocation in Stanly, and serve local job seekers is a significant contribution of the library to the region's welfare. Some of the changes that relate to advocacy include (1) a restructuring of public service (as mentioned previously, "outstanding public service" is a prerequisite of library advocacy efforts); (2) tracking data to report back to the corporate funder (accountability is a necessary component of successful advocacy; see chapter 7 and other discussions in this book); (3) the ability to instantly access the world at large, providing the community with an expanded vision that has positive implications for the library, including gratitude, dependence, and the fact that the more educated voters usually vote yes on library referenda); and (4) marketing the library's products, ensuring that the information about the library's resources gets to the people who need it. The downsides of the innovation—related expenses, maintenance, "technostress," and even a passing reference to censorship concerns—illustrate some of the costs of change that must be taken into account for the particular situation and community involved if advocacy initiatives are to be managed to advantage.

The library's task is to emphasize its community contributions, or assets, to public officials, providing them with, for example, a scenario of the situation that might result without the library's resources, giving quantitative data and dollar equivalents of the library's services, and offering firsthand reports from those who have been helped by the library's services where it counts, for example, in jobs and job skills.

Notes

1. Pat Ryckman, "About Libraries Online!" inset in Penny Welling, "Introducing the Internet in a Rural Setting," *North Carolina Libraries* (winter 1996), p. 166.

2. Greg Jaffe, "In a Region of Riches, County Loses Jobs, Hope," *Wall Street Journal,* January 31, 1996, p. S1.

Chapter 6

New System: Forty-Three Allegheny County (Pa.) Libraries

Today we are living through one of those exclamation points in history when the entire structure of human knowledge is once again trembling with change as old barriers fall.

—Alvin and Heidi Toffler, *The Politics of the Third Wave*
(Atlanta: Turner Publishing, 1995), p. 36

Changing to a new "governing system" is difficult for librarians in Allegheny County in the same way it is difficult for municipal officials and much of the population at large. Often there is a sense that moving to a more collaborative governing structure might compromise local autonomy.

—Marilyn A. Jenkins, Allegheny County library administrator

Total income of libraries: $7 million

In 1996, library officials of some forty municipal libraries in Allegheny County, Pennsylvania, met to consider whether to surrender a portion of their independence for membership in a federated system. Among other benefits, the system would favorably position the libraries for future funding. At this time, library budgets were at the mercy of deflated local economies following the collapse of the steel industry in western Pennsylvania that left public services, and especially libraries, among the bereaved.

At stake in the new system was (1) the support of a county tax board that had recently agreed to long-term library funding while encouraging system formation and (2) the possibility of other perks, such as increased contributions from the various municipalities and a countywide library tax. Because county tradition had always maintained separate municipalities (the only voluntary cooperative effort that was known to have crossed the borders was in the 1950s in the health industry), the possibility of library cooperation was a hard sell. In addition, the fact that library proceeds from the new county asset tax were already being distributed did not help advance the move toward federation because this biggest payoff of system formation was already a reality.

The plan for federation has, as its major priority, improved funding on the local and county levels. Included are efforts to equalize funding, to define strategies for planning and approaching old and new funding sources, to seek other countywide funding to supplement and eventually replace sporadic municipal funds, to pursue various marketing strategies to increase the viability of the libraries in their local economies, and to coordinate more efficient expenditure of monies funded through the asset tax board. In addition, a projected $50,000 in increased state funds is likely to be available annually to system members, according to Albert F. Kamper, district coordinator for the Allegheny County libraries.

With all the pluses that the new federated system offers, it would seem to those in the grandstand that the transition to its full acceptance would take place with no glitches. However, "the libraries do not want to be in a position where they are dictated to," said Kamper. "We try to assure them, but some are hard-nosed and won't believe us. It's a case of sitting down with them and giving examples of what it all means." Consequently, expectations that a year would be needed to work out the kinks increased to two years or more, as change would have it.

The two main areas of concern expressed by potential members according to Kamper were (1) dollars, as in, "Will we get more than we get now, or might we get less," or, "Will they take our dollars off the top to manage it?" and (2) control, as in, "Who's going to run it and think they'll tell us what to do?" The following remarks at a hearing for the federated system's draft proposal—open to all county librarians, library trustees, delegates, and the general public—illustrate these concerns and give some examples of the process of change. The objections that were expressed (these occupied most of discussion) dealt with a lack of interest in cooperating, the terms of the system's funding formula, a potential reduction in funding, administrative complexities, and "free rides" for unfunded municipalities:

> Our small municipality does not want to blend into a regional system; the socio-economics are different from surrounding communities—one of our minority group member trustees is opposed for this reason. We won't be wanting to go to their libraries, and they won't be wanting to come to ours. We have a levy and are well-supported locally. Our neighbors don't have a levy, their libraries aren't as good as ours.
>
> The funds that the new system will distribute depend on the size of the municipal contributions. It is not realistic to expect our municipality to give the library

more money when the police and fire departments and roads don't have adequate funding.

You'll be taking away our county money! Other municipalities will benefit from the money we are supposed to get but can't because our local funding board won't provide their share.

We'll have to deal with more people. What other administrative overhead might this lead to?

We need a way to get funding from the unfunded communities so that there won't be a drain on those of us who have funds.

Our library would lose money if it had to serve the whole county.

In support of system formation were the following statements:

We have to stop crying and feeling sorry for ourselves. Let's be the first in the county to work together. Boy, did we ever work together fast when the RAD dollars [asset tax proceeds] became possible.

Its time has come. This is about power and clout. We can't talk to the county without it.

The system is us. We can create whatever we want—so get on a committee if you have fears.

We got RAD funds in the first place by working hard. We must look at the big picture. "A house divided against itself cannot stand." [Abraham Lincoln, quoted]

A local councilman who also sat on a municipal library board weighed the pros and cons. On the one hand, the county tax board might require system membership at some point for libraries to receive funding; on the other hand, it was possible that the county funds "could dry up altogether." His conclusion: "We're waiting for an earth-shattering 'kaboom' to determine which way we'll go."

Favoring system membership for the distribution of foundation funds were the local foundations that funded the libraries' automation project (see chapter 2). Foundations "don't really want to deal with so many entities," said a spokesperson for a local foundation.

Kamper estimated that about half the county libraries would join when the system finally went into effect. A library director whose board was considering system membership apparently summed up the thoughts of several when he said, "It's better to cooperate. It's a lot easier to get money in groups than as individuals, and federation allows us to look at the collective picture better. We need better service in several areas of the county. It's possible the federated system could even this out and could deal, for example, with the situation of a library closing. Politically and financially there is more clout with the federated system. It will affect us. I'll have more paperwork and another library board meeting to attend."

Postscript: The system formation was approved in the summer of 1997, about a year and a half after initial efforts to organize had begun. Nearly two-thirds of the libraries voted to become members—more than those who followed the process of agreement had predicted. Kamper attributed the yes vote to support of the system concept in general and a "dwindling" of the opposition.

Comment

Ironically, the same municipal conservatism that opposes cooperative efforts also provided the dedicated efforts that built the various municipal libraries in the first place. However, efforts to preserve local authority are antithetical to the cooperation and interdependence on which library advocacy is based. Strength in numbers is a cornerstone of library advocacy: the numbers of entities involved in any single effort, the numbers of users of individual libraries, the numbers of postcards on council members' desks, and so on.

Chapter 7

Conclusion

Once something changes, it will never again be what it was before.

—Lucretius (d. 55 b.c.), quoted in Galen Rowell, "Climbing to Disaster," *Wall Street Journal,* May 29, 1997, p. A16

The previous chapters outline a number of principles of good library advocacy that are inherent, either by design or happenstance, in various changes that public libraries undergo. These principles of advocacy occur throughout the book in other contexts as well:

1. Outstanding public service
2. Collaborative efforts
3. Accountability to funders
4. Marketing new services to the public
5. Convincing the opposition
6. Attracting new donors
7. Building new facilities
8. Installing new technology
9. Increasing community awareness

As shown in the previous chapters, when library change is linked with library funding advocacy, the following take place:

1. The attention of funders and the community is intensified.
2. The media becomes involved.
3. The competition is overridden.
4. Opposition emerges, requiring skillful managing.
5. Library Friends increase in numbers.
6. The community mind-set influences how the library changes.

7. Advance planning facilitates the implementation of change.
8. Defining business objectives facilitates the implementation of change.
9. Efforts can be slowed by strong, conservative thinking.
10. Change requires more time than expected to implement.

More about change and advocacy is discussed in the chapters to come.

RULE 2

MOBILIZE THE TEAM (TEAMS FOR FUNDING ADVANTAGE)

Chapter 8

Introduction

Everybody's in on the fun. That's the nice thing about all this. Everyone is throwing a little something into the mix.

—Jim Leyland, manager of the Pittsburgh Pirates baseball team, in Ron Cook, "Pirates Extend Streak to 11," *Pittsburgh Post-Gazette,* September 23, 1996, p. C7

One of the most important elements about our library is that we all laugh a lot.

—Public library director, Long Island, New York

None of us is as smart as all of us.

—Phil Comdit, "Quotable Quotes," *Reader's Digest,* March 1997, p. 49

A team is a group of people who work together to achieve a common purpose for which they hold themselves collectively accountable. It is estimated that over a third of American businesses — mostly in the service sector — are using teams or similar strategies to solicit employee input for "how we can do it better."

Libraries also look to "how they can do it better" and find inspiration in the business world, mainly in long-range planning, political finesse, innovation, collaboration, and teamwork. Using concepts such as these is important because libraries want funds from business and business-structured public agencies. They position themselves more favorably using the language of business as a starting point to negotiation.

A team structure has several advantages for libraries. Because "two heads are better than one," teams can access more ideas, perform more tasks, and have a variety of energies, dynamics, and resources at their disposal. "Sometimes we're clean out of ideas," said a library fund-raiser. So what do they do then? "Get everybody together and brainstorm. We always come up with something." Ideas need refreshing from a pool of minds, and this is where the team comes in.

The Oxnard Public Library (see chapter 3) happens to be team managed. According to City Manager Tom Frutchey, the team structure, applied to all city departments in Oxnard, has the advantages of allowing staff full input into decisions and saving dollars in supervisory and administrative overhead. It also gives staff "ownership of resources and of customer satisfaction," said Frutchey, adding, "as the old saying goes, if you have your face to your boss, your backside is to your customers." Librarians no longer tolerate their backsides turned to customers—that went out with the card catalog—so teams might be an advantage.

Other advantages are that teams have a better chance to represent community sentiments than a person acting alone—an advantage to a community-based activity such as advocacy. Team members also encourage one another to achieve the team's objectives. In addition, the collective team structure helps sanction the activity, and team efforts can prevent an individual's doubt and timidity from hampering a process.

Teams also have disadvantages. They can take longer to make decisions than an individual does, team members might not be as knowledgeable as a single expert, and personality conflicts can mar the results. Also, team members must be diligent in the activities of the team for which they are collectively accountable. For example, had the team of board members of the infamous New Era Philanthropy been more diligent in the team's responsibility to the organization, illegal dealings that recently injured the financial nest eggs of several institutions, including public libraries, might have been avoided.[1]

Teams can also end up managing more than they were asked to manage (perhaps because they like their role so much?), and consequently open a "can of worms." This happened in a large urban library when a team found much more to investigate among management's activities than they were asked to investigate. Consequently, their recommendations were ignored.

All these aspects of a team structure can affect library advocacy teams. The field accounts in this chapter emphasize the following characteristics of library advocacy teams:

- The team has the objective of generating funds, conserving funds, or positioning the library favorably for funding.
- The goals of the team support the library's mission.
- The team employs various tools and practices identified with library advocacy as well as the necessary staff and resources to accomplish its objectives.
- Funds obtained as a result of the team's efforts benefit the library's programs or operations.

Teams come in all sizes relevant to their functions. In this chapter, teams range from two members for the direct soliciting of funds to thirty members for budget action.

Notes

1. Steve Stecklow, "Owing $500 Million, New Era Charity Seeks Refuge from Creditors," *Wall Street Journal,* May 16, 1995, p. A1.

Chapter 9

A Budget Action Team at the New York Public Library, the Branch Libraries

> The New York Public Library has incredibly effective lobbying efforts. Every year they explain to our staff the details of their programs—literacy resources, kid's reading, ribbon cuttings, and whatever, and how many people are using the library. The numbers are very important to them. They emphasize to us that people who like the library, vote.
>
> —Andrew Berman, assistant to New York City
> Council member Tom Duane

> We trained our staff how not to be afraid to talk to legislators.
>
> —Fran Nathan, retired legislative affairs manager,
> New York Public Library

Library income: $88.8 million
Local government share: 83 percent

For its long history in the otherwise short span of library advocacy, its mobilization of hundreds of grassroots volunteers, and its continuing success in gaining local funds for branch libraries, the New York Public Library's thirty-member Budget Action Committee (BAC) is a staff team effort that is unsurpassed. The committee dates back to the city's 1975 fiscal crisis, when forty of the library public staged a sit-in at the Columbia branch to protest funding cuts. According to Rick Lepkowski, manager of legislative affairs and a former political organizer, "Library administrators were so impressed with this mobilization of support that they asked how they could continue to harness this energy on the library's behalf."

This question set in motion several responses, including the establishment of the BAC, the objective of which is to implement a systemwide campaign for local funding of the branch libraries; the target for fiscal year 1997 was $67 million. (The system's research libraries, including the stone-lion-flanked landmark building at Fifth Avenue and Forty-second Street, are funded separately and, for the most part, privately.) The campaign targets city officials (i.e., council members, borough presidents, and the mayor), as 80 percent or more of branch libraries' public funds come from the city.

Members of the BAC, which meets five times per year, are mostly regional librarians who are supervisors of four or more branches and whose responsibilities on the BAC are to keep the branch libraries abreast of budget action priorities and to supervise their advocacy activities. These activities include setting up letter-writing tables staffed by volunteers, organizing visits to elected officials, hosting the officials at the branch libraries, and participating in many other activities spelled out in the library's *Budget Action Handbook,* a looseleaf reference manual with instructions for advocacy that is distributed to all professional staff (see its listings in appendix 2).

Above all, advocates keep in mind the needs of legislators. "Legislators want two things," said a former staff advocate, "money and votes. How can the library show its support in hopes of reciprocation? We would create events for council members to meet voters at the library, and when we'd have a lecture with thirty to forty persons expected, we'd phone our council member in case he or she wanted to come."

"What's important is continual effort . . . getting our message heard throughout the process," said Lepkowski. Advocacy starts in the fall, when the community boards (see chapter 5) develop their budgets. "After the mayor releases the preliminary budget in January," said Lepkowski, "we encourage our volunteers to set up letter-writing tables for library users to write to city council and ask for more dollars in the budget. When a user comes to the reference desk to ask for help, the librarian points out the letter-writing table, saying something like, 'By the way, at that table over there are letter-writing materials for you to write and tell the mayor how important the library is to you.'" Handwritten postcards rather than form letters are sent, and a jar is provided for cash contributions to postage.

Lepkowski described how library advocates top off their efforts at the end of the campaign. In the final days of the campaign, city council members are met in the morning at city hall by the president of the library and the vice president for government affairs. They are reminded, "Don't forget the library." Upstairs in their offices, council members find on their desks 200 postcards from constituents variously inscribed, "Don't forget the library." In the afternoon they go to their district offices to meet constituents from the neighborhood branch support group with the same refrain, "Don't forget the library." Finally, at night they go to a community meeting to meet library staff from their local branches with the (it is hoped) never-to-be-forgotten message, "Don't forget the library."

Council member Ronnie Eldridge said, "The libraries have done a wonderful job of political organizing. I use them as examples for other lobbying organizations. We all get letters, scrapbooks with detailed information. . . . I think we feel that if the mayor doesn't budget for the library, the council will add funds because council has this discretionary power."

Council regularly adds funds. In the fiscal year 1997 campaign, it restored $3.1 million in discretionary funds to the mayor's library budget to continue six-day-a-week service in all branches and the research centers, to prevent cuts to the materials budget and several programs, and to fund forty new capital improvement projects, among other things.[1]

The major campaign emphasis in the 1990s was to extend library hours and keep them extended. In fiscal year 1992, the library went from four to five days and in fiscal year 1993 from five to six days. "It's tangible," said Andrew Berman, staff assistant to council member Tom Duane, "something the average person on the street will recognize. Hours are especially important to seniors and children because their time to visit the library is usually restricted."

However, the question of an adequate materials budget is still at large. "We were premature in opening branch libraries to six days a few years ago," said Eldridge, "because we didn't have enough money for books to have libraries open that long, and still don't. Librarians thought so too but couldn't say it. It's a political symbol to have the libraries open."

The biggest scores by the BAC for fiscal year 1997 were $1.2 million to expand CLASP (the Connecting Libraries and Schools Project) and $2.6 million to upgrade the telecommunications infrastructure for the library's LEO computer system. CLASP, a program that encourages reading in the local school districts, is a collaborative effort of the three public library systems serving New York City besides the New York Public Library, the Queens Borough Public Library, and the Brooklyn Public Library. For the first three years, CLASP was funded privately by the DeWitt Wallace-Reader's Digest Fund in twenty-three New York Public Library branches and 107 public schools.[2] At the end of the pilot period, it was deemed so successful that, at the library's recommendation, the city council provided support to begin the phase-in of the program in all branches of the city's libraries.

As the library's initial Internet access did not include the Web, in 1996 the BAC pushed for capital funds to provide T-1 lines in each branch to accommodate additional hardware. "We got our public officials to the branches for a demonstration of the new system—city council had just created its own Web page—so we pulled up their pictures," said Lepkowski. In addition, this issue was discussed at community board meetings. Each of the library representatives went to the community board with a capital budget for the upgrade and invited council members and their staff for demonstration classes, showing how the Web would help them. The response was "overwhelmingly positive," said Lepkowski, partly because "enthusiasm was still riding on the thrust of the kickoff for the Internet in November 1995," and "we always try to give credit to the people who make the funds possible." The original LEO system was paid for by discretionary funds from the Manhattan borough president and the mayor.

"Council members already know our needs because they see us at the community boards," said Lepkowski. " We're not educating them but reinforcing the consistent message they've received from us for the past eight months. If advocacy were only at the end of the legislative session when all the chips are down, we wouldn't do as well."

Comment

This field account illustrates the process of political advocacy in the third-largest public library in the United States (the Los Angeles City and County libraries are the first and second largest, respectively).[3] Important to the team effort is its being founded in response to a community need, its broad-based representation of library interests, and its generous interpretation of means to the ends (e.g., making efforts early in the legislative process and searching for ways to help the council members with their own needs for publicity). Tools of advocacy are budget presentations, community letter writing, one-to-one interactions with funders, and the bargaining chips familiar to libraries from New York to California: open hours and materials budgets. Also significant is the response from council members, who see themselves as partners who recognize the efforts of the library to get itself funded, and the council's role in the effort. A final hallmark of library advocacy is the endurance required in touching all the bases with as many means as possible and being there in person.

The two field accounts under rule 5 (chapters 33 and 36) are relevant to this one and give additional insight into the environment in which the BAC operates.

Notes

1. New York Public Library, The Branch Libraries, "Memorandum," July 10, 1996.

2. New York Public Library et al., "CLASP" (Connecting Libraries and School Project), brochure, June 1995, 9 pp.

3. Public Library Association, *Statistical Report '97* (Chicago: ALA, 1997).

Chapter 10

A Cost-Cutting Team at the Chicago Public Library

> You form a special bond with your teammates because they're like family. When the season's over, it's like you lost your arm or part of your body.
>
> —Kevin Polcovich of the Pittsburgh Pirates baseball team, quoted in Robert Dvorchak, "A Baseball Season to Cherish," *Pittsburgh Post-Gazette,* October 21, 1997, special section, p. 2

> We felt we were comrades going through the fire together.
>
> —Diane Richmond, co-team leader and librarian, Science and Technology Information Center, Chicago Public Library

Library income: $71.1 million
Local government share: 85 percent

Not only are funds actively sought by libraries, but the ones already in hand can be actively conserved. Such was the goal of a team of employees at the Chicago Public Library that cut the number of steps spent processing a book to one-third, saving the library thousands of dollars per year in staff hours. Following training in 1993 in a government-sponsored Total Quality Management (TQM) program (a Government Assistance Program, or GAP, established by the Chicago Community Trust to examine the efficiency of public services[1]), the team addressed several problems in book processing. "Everybody considered book processing the Moby Dick of the library," said a team member.[2] By eliminating the individual processing of books by the system's eighty-six branch libraries (each of which used a different processing method) and by streamlining procedures, the team was able to make a number of changes in the logistics of a book from time of receipt from a dealer to checkout by a borrower. Some of these were the following:

- *Processing.* The time spent processing a single book was reduced from 32 steps outlined in three flowcharts to 11 steps outlined in one flowchart.
- *Preparation for checkout.* The time required for preparing a single book for checkout was reduced from 22.8 or more working days to 10.5 days.
- *Delivery time to branch library.* The delivery time from the drop-off points to the branch libraries was reduced from 7.5 working days on average to 1 working day or less.
- *Availability.* The availability in the central library was reduced from several months later than the branches to same time as the branches.
- *Backlog.* The backlog of books in the book processing department went from a 36-truck backlog to a 4-truck backlog, a 90 percent improvement.

The changes that were implemented reduced the required steps in book processing from 172 to 81, a 53 percent reduction in the workload.[3]

"It was a physically and emotionally draining effort," said a team member, "and none of our other duties were removed . . . we were hurtled down the corridor." Using fishbone and root-cause diagrams and other TQM techniques, the team was up two or three nights at the onset of their training, analyzing the book processing system.

Team members (nine in all) were drawn from a wide range of staff, including a children's librarian, an acquisitions department assistant, the head of book processing, the head of cataloging, a district chief in charge of twenty branches, and the head of the library's Science and Technology Information Center. Two clerical staff and a training and development officer were also on the team.

The team expressed praise both for their efforts and for TQM. Co-team leader Diane Richmond, head of the library's Science and Technology Information Center, praised TQM as a tool for dealing with quantifiable data. "It's user friendly and disarms all the emotional commitment to the issues. The team could accomplish what no other individual—only the top echelon—has the authority to do. We made sweeping changes." Co-team leader Patty Novak was quoted in GAP's newsletter, saying, "It's so reassuring to know there are so many good, smart people who were willing to work so hard on the team and who were really excited by it."[4]

The GAP program, which provided the team's training from private funding, included basic ground rules, team-building exercises, and techniques in handling potential interpersonal conflicts. The hierarchy concept was out, and "rank had no privilege," said one member.

In addition to eliminating unnecessary processing steps, saving thousands of dollars of staff time at the library, the team made additional recommendations for eliminating certain applications being provided by the book distributor. If implemented, these recommendations could result in a savings of 30 percent, or $15,000 per 100,000 books from the distributor.[5]

However, the real gain was expressed by Richmond. "We feel the benefits every day. People ask for a book, and it's there. That's the most tangible product."

Comment

Efforts to use funds efficiently have an advocacy component in that they demonstrate, to the assurance of funders (in this case, city government, which initiated the TQM training program), that the library is committed to conserving the funds for which it advocates. This account illustrates the dedication with which the task was approached, the preparation that was required, and the mutual support of team members, all of which are characteristic of advocacy efforts.

Notes

1. Government Assistance Program (GAP), "Factsheet," The Egan Urban Center, DePaul University, Chicago (n.d.).

2. Government Assistance Program (GAP), *One for the Books* (newsletter), spring 1995 (photocopy provided by GAP).

3. Chicago Public Library, "Result of Book Processing Pilot," unpublished report, December 1993.

4. Government Assistance Program (GAP), *One for the Books* (photocopy provided by GAP).

5. Chicago Public Library, "Result of Book Processing Pilot."

Chapter 11

A Team of Two to Tap Foundations at the Carnegie Library of Pittsburgh

> The train is pulling out of the station. It will leave without you if you don't get aboard.

> —Frank J. Lucchino, county controller, addressing 140 municipal library representatives at a meeting to consider adoption of the Electronic Information Network (EIN) project, Allegheny County, Pennsylvania, December 1993

> In Pittsburgh, it is the foundation community whose power provides the drive. Once they identify you as a team player, they'll help you.

> —Loretta O'Brien, deputy director, Carnegie Library of Pittsburgh

Library income: $17.4 million
Local government share: 81 percent

In Pittsburgh, Pennsylvania, a team of two, representing the Carnegie Library of Pittsburgh (CLP) and the local government, joined forces to raise $10 million from local private foundations and corporations. The goal was based on the projected cost of the Electronic Information Network (EIN), a project to link some forty Allegheny County libraries with the Internet.

In the fall of 1994, a year of groundwork had already been laid by the three partners involved: the Carnegie Library of Pittsburgh, the Allegheny County Library Association, and the Commission on the Future of Libraries in Allegheny County. They had commissioned a feasibility study for the project—which turned into a 200-page, mostly technical report—funded by the Buhl

Foundation in Pittsburgh. They had also planned their strategy and taken two initial steps. The first step targeted six of the city's best-known and most influential foundations, hosting them at a breakfast presentation at Pittsburgh's elite Duquesne Club. The next step took place four months later, when forty-six members of the Grantmakers of Western Pennsylvania were invited to a library presentation. The foundations involved were the primary local funders serving the various municipalities, whose local funding bases had eroded while the western Pennsylvania steel industry was collapsing during the previous twenty-five years.

Of those who attended the breakfast presentation (about half of the invited), enthusiasm was immediate. "It was what they were looking for," said Bette Ann Hubbard, library development officer. Frank J. Lucchino, county commissioner and an ardent library supporter and chair of the Commission on the Future of Libraries in Allegheny County, said, "The foundations saw enormous benefit for the county—the cooperation of some forty or more municipal libraries. The funders were always looking to the advantages of cooperative efforts."

The project was positioned well from the beginning, having the support of both the county commissioner and the prestigious Buhl Foundation, which funded the feasibility study and hosted the library's initial meetings with foundations. The Buhl Foundation was attracted to the project partly because of its interest in innovative and pioneering projects, said president Doreen Boyce. The foundation had already funded automation efforts at the college and university libraries in the area, and it seemed a logical next step to extend similar resources to the public.

In addition, the concept of a regional system that contributed to the area's economic infrastructure, helping to "bring it up where it should be technologically," was such a special situation that the foundation did what it rarely, if ever, had done on behalf of a project: It alerted the other foundations in the region. "We usually respect each others' independent viewpoints in the foundation world," said Boyce. However, the significance of this project, and the fact that the foundation knew that very little state funding and probably only a small portion of county funding would be available, meant that the private sector would need to be the principal fund bearers. Among other things, this called for convincing foundations that did not fund libraries that this was not really a library project but a regional asset effort that deserved their consideration.

Finally, the Buhl Foundation was attracted to the project because it was a cooperative effort. If the foundation would not need to consider library automation proposals from forty separate systems, it could focus its resources more effectively.

Following the library's initial steps and the interest raised, Hubbard and Lucchino's administrative assistant, Beverly Blankowski, teamed up as representatives of the library and the county government to nail the funds. They had tried this before. "We discussed the EIN concept a few years ago," said

Blankowski, who brought to the team big-league experience as a political campaign manager and fund-raiser. "Everyone liked the idea, but they went back to their workplaces and forgot about it." This time they were not going to forget. "We put on our hats," said Blankowski, and went to bat for the project.

As Hubbard described the job, "We split the list of forty-six foundations in half, made phone calls to the head persons to set up appointments, dressed ourselves up, and with the generic proposal in hand [an eleven-page summary of the feasibility study] made the rounds. We also made presentations at foundation board meetings and occasionally took Dan Eddings [CLP project technician] with us. But we found that funders were not usually interested in a technical level of conversation."

Blankowski, who said that they researched the giving histories of the invitees to style their requests appropriately, said, "We were able to get appointments with almost everyone. It was not so much interest in EIN but because of the background of it—forty libraries that had had a reputation for thinking 'mine' instead of 'ours' and had held back library development in this area as a result—compared to, say, Cleveland and other cities. Now these libraries were finally working together."

Added Blankowski, "We took maps along with color-coded libraries showing which were state funded and which weren't and also the sites of the commission's projects [one of the partners; see chapter 7]. We told them that our goal was to connect all these. It caught their attention."

In return, foundation representatives wanted to know about the people who were managing the project, how it would be updated and maintained, how staff and users would be trained, how the project would help library management, and who else was funding it and in what amounts. They also wanted photos of the library and details on its background. Because this was the first venture of the library into the world of private funding, it was a learning experience for all concerned.

Potential funders also wanted some guarantee that the municipal libraries would buy into the project. This was apparently satisfied when the benefits were explained; that is, remote, rural areas would be linked up with the resources of all the other county libraries and, finally, with the world through the Internet.

Some funders called for a second meeting "to tailor various segments of the project," said Hubbard, "so we tied project goals into what particular funders wanted for regional development, emphasizing, for example, economics, medicine, and women's health issues. We also learned what the foundation protocol here is—the program officers called me to discuss, while the top persons called Bob [director Robert Croneberger]," said Hubbard.

Some funders confused the library's request with its parent organization's (the Carnegie Institute) stating, "We just funded you." (Traditionally, the library is funded from public funds, whereas the institute's two museums are funded privately, according to the terms of donor Andrew Carnegie's gift.)

In another case, a corporation had to be persuaded that the project deserved to be funded as an "educational/economic development/lifelong learning project," said Hubbard, and not in its usual category for libraries (i.e., "cultural activities"), which would not have permitted the funding, or not in the amount requested.

Most of the visits went well. Occasionally, "Someone would interrupt us in midsentence and say something like, 'cut that,' and it would throw us off, or we'd stand by the elevator afterwards and say, 'Darn, I blew that, forgot to mention our research.' But usually we'd say 'that went okay,' and we'd feel we had been well received," said Blankowski.

The final score of the team's efforts included eleven Pittsburgh foundations that contributed $9.2 million. Among these were the Buhl Foundation, the Vira I. Heinz Endowment, the R. K. Mellon Foundation, and the Hillman Foundation, Inc.; a few corporations also donated about 10 percent of the total. An additional pledge of $1.2 million in two installments came from county government.

"This was an opportunity to do something never done here before," said Hubbard. "Foundations needed to be educated about the library. We hadn't asked them before; maybe that's why they considered us more seriously."

Commenting on the team effort, Blankowski said, "Raising funds is always easier when you have someone pushing you. Bette Ann and I worked together well because we brought different styles that complemented each other—I was the pushy one and usually started out the presentation. A successful team effort involves "credibility," she said. "You speak the truth, not just what they want to hear. And you have a worthwhile product—one you believe in." Would they do anything different in retrospect? "It would have been nice to have had a dedicated effort," said Blankowski. "But we each had our regular jobs to do as well. If we could have concentrated just on the project, we could have raised more."

Comment

This discussion involves a project that has all the ingredients of a winning advocacy effort. First, as an initiative that has implications for the welfare of the region, it immediately earns the support of local movers and shakers: government and the foundation community. Second, it offers funders the advantage of easing their workload because they no longer need to be concerned with so many entities seeking funding. Third, the timing is right in that the funding foundation is primed to expand its initial automation efforts. Finally, the groundwork is carefully laid in the manner of successful advocacy efforts.

This account relates other qualities of successful library advocacy efforts as well: dedication, team member support, carefully executed persuasive tactics, and one-to-one relationships.

Chapter 12

Teams for Long-Range Planning at the Anderson Public Library, Anderson, Indiana; Fargo Public Library, Fargo, North Dakota; Reuben Hoar Public Library, Littleton, Massachusetts; and Orrville Public Library, Orrville, Ohio

> Among our winners, the team is the critical factor, regardless of the issue — service, innovation or productivity.
>
> —Thomas J. Peters and Robert H. Waterman Jr., *In Search of Excellence: Lessons from America's Best-Run Companies* (New York: Harper & Row, 1982), p. 275

Income: $3 million (Anderson P.L.), $1.1 million (Fargo P.L.), $600,000 (Orrville P.L.), $228,000 (Reuben Hoar P.L.)

Four public libraries of varying sizes have learned that long-range plans are valuable tools in funding and advocacy. "When we refer to our long-range plan, there is something about it that gets people's — and funders' — attention," said Susan Akers of the Anderson Public Library in Anderson, Indiana, which has had its long-range five-year plan in operation for three years. The plan was put together by a team consisting of the library's five-member board of directors (appointed by local public officials); the library director and associate director; department heads for technology, reference, and audiovisual; and a local university consultant.

When the Fargo Public Library in Fargo, North Dakota, started work on its recently completed long-range plan, it advertised in the community for citizen participation and got a few takers, according to library director Nann Blaine Hilyard. With a thought to "bolstering the library's position with the city," a city staff member—the mayor's executive assistant—was invited and then joined.

In addition, the library issued invitations to two library users who were, well, troublemakers of sorts. One of these users complained about the library's inadequacies compared to the library in the city he had just left (with a more generous budget). In other ways, this user did not have what a library director usually looks for in assembling a congenial team. The team, which met monthly for nine months, had as its first assignment distributing and collecting community output measure surveys with the help of volunteers. In the process, "they got to see how busy the library is—to observe it almost from the position that we on the staff do," said Hilyard, who thinks that this exercise also helped them forge a relationship with one another for a more effective team. Another important part of the effort was assigning two nonstaff persons to assist each library department head in writing the goals and objectives for that department so that the community link extended to the entire process.

Community members of the long-range-plan committee for the Reuben Hoar Library in Littleton, Massachusetts, outnumbered library representatives by 150 percent. The committee included six townspeople, two trustees, and two library staff. Although library director Marnie Oakes said that it was a bit "scary" at first, by the third meeting, when the community reps started referring to the library as "we," she knew that they were on the right track.

The plan has been completed only a few months, yet the library has already reaped some funding benefits that were "able to happen because people were talking about it," said Oakes, referring to a needed elevator that the town provided and a move toward funding Sunday hours. Both requests came from a community survey (completed before the plan was completed) that also emphasized the need to "conserve what we already have." This was the second long-range plan that the library developed; such plans are prerequisites to receiving state aid in Massachusetts.

In addition to involving community residents on the long-range-plan committee, the plan has a provision that the library intends to work with the community at large. Such an objective is included as well in the Anderson Public Library's plan, launched in 1993, to "develop partnerships with organizations and institutions to link the community to all available resources for lifelong learning, discovery, and enjoyment." This objective outlines ways in which each department agrees to support the objective. These included inviting library users to attend reference department meetings once a year for the library "to gather different perspectives on our services," and meeting with the public schools regarding "present and potential electronics and organizational linkages" and with "Economic Development and Chamber of Commerce to explore avenues of cooperation (e.g., electronic services)."

As one library director pointed out, "If you lay out your intentions this way, it's more likely you'll get them done." At least it worked for Anderson. The library joined in partnering with the local school system in a $2.3 million grant from the State Department of Education and the state library to establish a community technology center. Over 300 persons are trained in computer use and Internet access each month. "It's important," said Akers, "that the library not be an island, that we not stereotype ourselves, and that we initiate relationships with others who will see us as the vital center that we are." Furthermore, she said, the library makes sure that it knows its community—a blue-collar factory town of 70,000, "not real educated"— for whom the video and CD collection, for example, is especially important.

Speaking for the Madison County Community Foundation, which has provided funding to the library on several occasions, Jeannie Lee, executive director, said that "it gives us a sense of security when an organization is looking ahead. We see a lot of nonprofits with good intentions but no plan of action. Ultimately, projects fall apart when they are not connected with a mission. The library spent a long time in preparing its plan and gave considerable thought to it. Having this broad-based support helped them turn a corner for themselves. They have also established an endowment, which very likely came out of the long-range planning. The endowment has attracted several inquiries concerning bequests."

Also with a stake in the community, the Orrville Public Library in Orrville, Ohio, completed a long-range plan a year ago, included the president of the library Friends on the committee, and did a community survey to gain further insight into what the library's objectives should be. It also looked at national trends in general (not only library trends) and came up with such facts as the popularity of prepackaging in our culture (e.g., buying salad in a bag instead of buying all the ingredients separately to assemble yourself). This observation inspired a proposal for preparing materials for school programs for which the library received an LSCA (Library Services Construction Act) grant. "It may not be advocacy exactly," said library director Lynn Stainbrook, "but it impressed our Friends [that we would consider this kind of input], and it makes them better advocates for the library."

In the meantime, Fargo has presented its new plan to the city council "just to show them what good stewards we are," said Hilyard.

Comment

This account illustrates how a long-range plan fits into the library's advocacy efforts by (1) involving the community as committee members, (2) facilitating private and public funding, and (3) incorporating objectives that confirm the library's commitment to community initiatives, such as partnerships.

Chapter 13

Conclusion

Chicago and New York are lit up by games no one thought they would ever see.

—Photo caption, *Pittsburgh Post-Gazette,* June 17, 1997, Sports and Business section, p. B1

The field accounts in the previous chapters describe outside team efforts (i.e., soliciting private foundations and local council members) as well as teams working inside the library to develop long-range plans and strategies for cutting costs in service delivery. The following tools of library advocacy are used:

- Cooperative efforts
- Community input
- Community welfare concerns
- Business-related tactics
- Publicity about the library's efforts
- Mutual support for more effective results
- Dedicated efforts
- Advance preparation to touch all the bases
- Prudent timing
- Tactful persuasion
- Cultivation of personal relationships
- One-to-one interactions with funders
- Budget presentations
- Community letter writing
- Volunteer labor
- Frequent visits to city council members

Using these techniques, the teams were able to obtain new funds or position the library favorably for future funding by conserving current funds and through long-term planning.

For Advocacy Teams: Lessons from Flying Geese

"Solidarity: Lessons from Geese," attributed to Ryugen Fisher, of Rhinelander, Wisconsin, is a prose piece that appeared in the newsletter of the Pennsylvania Library Association. To apply its lessons to teams for advocacy, it is adapted as follows:

Fact 1: As each goose flaps its wings, it creates an uplift for the bird that follows. By flying in a "V" formation, the whole flock adds 71 percent greater flying range than if each bird flew alone. *Advocacy lesson:* One team member facilitates another so that the team as a whole has far greater capability than individual members.

Fact 2: When a goose falls out of formation, it suddenly feels the drag and resistance of flying alone. It quickly moves back into formation to take advantage of the lifting power of the bird immediately in front of it. *Advocacy lesson:* A library advocate notices the difference between going it alone and going with a team and wisely opts for the latter.

Fact 3: When the lead goose tires, it rotates back into formation, and another goose flies to the point position. *Advocacy lesson:* The usual physical drawbacks do not interfere with the success of a cooperative team effort.

Fact 4: The geese flying in formation honk to encourage those up front to keep up their speed. *Advocacy lesson:* A team member cannot forget that it has responsibility to other members of the team as well as their support in playing one's part.

Fact 5: When a goose gets sick, wounded, or shot down, two geese drop out of formation and follow it down to help and protect it. They stay with it until it dies or is able to fly again. Then they launch out with another formation or catch up with the flock. *Advocacy lesson:* Team members recognize how special each member of the team is and offer their support even when the worst happens.

RULE 3

PARTNER WITH CLOUT (PARTNERSHIPS FOR FUNDING ADVANTAGE)

Chapter 14

Introduction

Library partnership—A contract entered into by a library and one or more other organizations in which each agree to furnish a part of the capital, labor or other resources for a project of common interest or activity and each shares in whatever profits and losses — monetary or otherwise—are generated as a result.

—Adapted from "partnership" in *The Heritage Illustrated Dictionary of the English Language*

Clout—A long powerful hit in baseball. Power, prestige, or influence; pull; political clout.

—*The Heritage Illustrated Dictionary of the English Language*

A major increase in library partnerships has occurred in the last decade, largely as a result of library outreach for funding purposes. Funders like partnerships because they conserve and multiply resources, consolidate efforts physically and administratively, and provide a broader constituency for developing ideas and managing a project, all of which improve the chances of a project's success. Additional advantages are obtained through funders. They enable the library to see itself through the eyes of its community partners, to clarify the library's mission, to advocate it more widely, to pave the way for more partnerships, and to enlarge the base of community support that tips the scales for public and private funding.

When libraries partner with an organization that is well positioned in the community by reason of political, social, or business influence—or clout (as in the accounts in the following chapters)—the library, by association, increases its own political, social, and business connections. It also receives attention where it might have had little or none and earns a reputation for being a team player on its home turf. These are qualities valued in the public and private funding sectors. Through partnerships, the library can sharpen up its reputation in the community.

Partnerships require careful planning, preparation, and constant attention if they are to succeed. No library wants a failed partnership, as it can result in bad feelings, negative publicity, and loss of faith in those whom one would rather not offend. In one case, an urban public library known for its astute partnerships with educational organizations had a partnership with a major regional bank that lent its products to the library. It soon became clear that the bank insisted on the library's use of these products exclusively while the library wanted to use competing products as well. As the library's mission was "educational, not marketing the bank's products," said a library official, it opted out of the partnership, conceding that the area of for-profit partnerships was a whole different ball of string that it had not yet unraveled.

In the case of a failed partnership between a public library and a community college with a government contract, the community college initiated a competing project, causing "a war" between the two operations. Because the library was a junior partner, as viewed by the funders, and not a signatory agent to the project, the funders sided with the college, and the library lost its share of the project funding. What did the library learn from this? That it should always look at the way the prospective partner is "growing," said the librarian, or how it is increasing its scope and services. "Is it by conquering or by cooperating?" Too late, the library discovered that its partner was "a conqueror who had nailed a few other partners in the process." Other advice from the library was that the parties should know and like each other and should write a contract with tight language (i.e., be specific: "Forbid people to set up another shop.").

Libraries need not experience a failed partnership to learn the necessary lessons. The following accounts illustrate successful partnerships that benefit library funding directly or that position the library to funding advantage. Characteristics of these partnerships are introduced as follows:

- Groundwork for the partnership is laid so that before any agreements are made, the library makes a dedicated effort to become acquainted with the partner, its institutional mission, its objectives in the proposed partnership, and the specific resources that it is prepared to bring to the partnership.
- The partnership is expected to generate funds for the library or to position the library favorably for funding whether or not this is the partnership's main objective.
- The goals of the partnership fit well with the missions of the library and its partner.
- The process for achieving the goals is initiated and controlled by the partners in a well-planned and dedicated effort.

- Funds or other benefits as an outcome of the partnership are leveraged into funds, materials, publicity, or other advantages for the library (or into all these).

The conclusion in chapter 21 expands these guidelines on the basis of information from the following accounts of current library practices.

Chapter 15

Partnering with Political Clout: Oakland Public Library, Oakland, California

> We both want the same thing—funding of library services. Wages are only a small part. If the state and city don't fund, we don't have a job.
>
> —Ray Markey, president, Local 1930, New York Public Library
> Guild, Professional and Cultural Division, American
> Federation of State, County and Municipal Employees, AFL-CIO

Library income: $11.7 million
Local government share: 97 percent

When the Friends of the Oakland Public Library (FOL) in Oakland, California, initiated the campaign for parcel tax Measure O in an attempt to recover the defeat they had suffered with an earlier version, they chose to include Local 790 of the Service Employees International Union (SEIU) early in the planning stage. In the earlier campaign, the union had come aboard late in the game. It was a good strategy for a politically oriented city where, for example, a local architect had refused to lend his support to the campaign because a library building project had not hired an Oakland architect.

The union was an ideal partner for the Friends group. It brought political savvy to the venture as a result of its "tremendous role" in electing city council members and the continuing "power and influence" it exercised, according to Margaret E. Cunningham, SEIU field representative for ten years. In addition, union officials had already worked with the library's campaign manager (whom they helped select) on "a number of previous campaigns for school board and city council candidates." As a general principle, said Cunningham, the union believes in working for public funding of public facilities because successful efforts add to the total funding that is available to the city in general.

As expected, each partner had its own interest in a successful outcome. The library would gain more secure library service—including increases in hours of opening, the book budget, children's librarians, and various programs—and the union would have a more stable funding base for its members that included, as it still does, all but the top administration of library employees. The union would also boost its image by joining with a "relatively respected community group—the FOL," said Terry Preston, FOL executive director, "and help blunt criticism of the union that it was interested more in worker comfort than public service."

Cunningham described the major role of the union in the campaign:

Before the campaign began, a phone survey of Oakland voters was conducted to determine the importance of library services compared to other services and to get a picture of how much the public would be willing to pay for a library assessment. The survey was conducted out of our Local offices. I participated, as did many of our library members. I remember that Martin Gomez, the library director at that time, stopped by every night to lend moral support and that it was one of the few times a department head had been in our offices. . . . Those phone-bank evenings helped consolidate our excellent ongoing working relationship with the library.

In addition to participating on the steering committee, we also helped with the work of the campaign. One effort was a huge mailing to voters. It took about a week of intense effort by many Local 790 library members, library management, and members of Friends of the Oakland library to get the mailing out.

We also provided money to the campaign—probably $1000, the limit under campaign laws.

Our primary effort, however, was in phone banking. For several weeks we had phone banks running out of our office almost every weeknight. There would be five to ten phoners calling on behalf of Measure O every night. Again, some would be management, some Friends, some members. Union staff, usually . . . and I, were on hand to host, provide scripts and other duplicated materials, order food, clean up, and help phone. This was in addition to our other campaign efforts, which included support of the mayor's reelection. All of our Oakland phone-banking scripts included a Measure O piece, so in the weeks immediately preceding the elections, other Oakland 790 members were also calling on behalf of the measure.

We also carried Measure O literature in our precinct-walking efforts on behalf of the mayor. On one or two weekends just before the election, we participated in a major signage effort, putting up "Yes on Measure O" signs all over the city. Our phone-banking efforts included requests to voters to put up signs.

The Measure O campaign was featured in our written communications to members about voting. Our bimonthly union newspaper, *The United Worker,* provides a voting guide before the election, and we also send a letter to members about important campaigns. We distribute *The United Worker* and compact card-sized voting guides to members through our workplace distribution systems.

Finally, Measure O was part of the phoning efforts of the Alameda Central Labor Council, which, because of our endorsement, also endorsed the measure. The
Labor Council runs phone banks three or four nights a week during campaign sea-
son, with members from AFL-CIO unions from all over the county. It also publishes
a voting guide in its publication, *The East Bay Labor Journal,* which goes out to
thousands of union members in Alameda County, many of whom live in Oakland.

Preston attributed the success of the FOL-SEIU partnership to "bringing the
union in early and treating it like an equal partner and making sure that union,
management, and community groups engage in common work, not having each
group 'do their own thing,' even if for a common goal."

Partnering with a union to secure funding is also done successfully in New
York City. For example, the New York Public Library considers Local 1930 of
the American Federation of State, County and Municipal Employees, AFL-
CIO, a "key component" of the library's budget process. The union discusses
budget action strategies at their local meetings, briefs staff members who might
otherwise not have access to the information, and develops ways in which the
union can participate in these strategies, said staff member Rick Lepkowski.
Citing a typical example of the union's help, he said,

A couple of years back, our union rep, Ray Markey, identified a union member—
a librarian—to speak in support of libraries at a city council budget hearing. The
library had just hired dozens of new librarians, many from other parts of the country, when service was expanded to five and six days. The message this young librarian gave to the city council was that "many of us came from other parts of the
country to work and live in New York. We love New York, and if the library's
budget is cut, we could lose our jobs."

Apparently, the plea worked. Hours were not cut, and jobs were retained.

Lepkowski said that the most important thing about union partnering, in his
opinion, was "the message it sends to unionized staff. If the union leadership is
involved in budget action work and makes it a priority, then union members—
librarians in our branches—are more likely to think, 'Hey, I need to make this
a priority.'"

As in the Oakland partnership, the professional connections that the union
has can be especially helpful to the library. The fact that the library's union rep-
resents thousands of city workers in hundreds of different jobs, said Lepkowski,
means that the library's rep can hear what other local presidents are saying
about the budget and how it is affecting their members. This, in turn, can affect
the library's budget strategy. "If, for example, other agencies are receiving significant cuts while the library is not slated for cuts, we have toned down our
message. [Consequently,] our union rep's 'ear' is very important to us in the
development of strategy."

Commenting on the subsequent Oakland partnership, Preston said that since the successful 1994 campaign, the FOL has helped the union in a public relations campaign to "humanize" its image to city residents. However, after that, "things waned a bit. The union didn't support the FOL when the FOL fought what it believed was a too-hefty administrative surcharge on the voter-approved library fund. The union wanted as much money as possible going to the general fund to protect all workers. Nor did the union strongly support a recent effort to adopt a bond measure for safer public facilities, concentrating on local council races instead." The failure to support the latter was due, in Preston's opinion, to the fact that "no jobs were likely to be immediately lost if the bond measure failed."

Comment

This account illustrates one of the requirements of successful partnerships: that each partner's mission be taken into account. As long as the library's goals are the same as the union's (as in the campaign for funds that has implications for jobs), the partnership works. Subsequent efforts are not successful because each partner has different goals.

The library Friends, which manages the referendum campaign, partners with the union because of the resources the union can bring to the campaign: political activism and a track record in working on successful referenda campaigns, experience working with the library's campaign manager, extensive contacts in the community (including the city council), and the necessary labor and resources for phone banks, mailings, and other publicity. In other words, the union satisfies a number of the library's needs, making it a worthy partner.

Other benefits of this partnership are the bonding formed early on between a number of members of the two groups as they work together on the phone surveys and the support and active interest of the library's top administrator. The library-union partnership illustrates the union's ability to rally librarians in the campaign and unique ways in which the union contributes to the partnership's goals using its community connections.

Chapter 16

Partnering with Community Clout: Rochester Hills Public Library, Rochester Hills, Michigan

> The chance encounter, the conversation in the corridor, meeting for lunch—that's what sparks projects. Menus and e-mail don't have human contact.
>
> —Julie Yamamuto, "Getty Center Paints Rosy Future,"
> *San Francisco Chronicle,* July 15, 1996, p. D2

Library income: $2.7 million
Local government share: 84 percent

Before launching its annual drive one year, the Rochester Hills Public Library in Rochester, Michigan—an area of wooded hills on the edge of Detroit's urban sprawl—was advised by a professional fund-raiser that in order to raise more than the penny-ante the library was currently raising, the library director "must travel in the circuit where the big dollars are." These circles hold the promise of partnering opportunities that can leverage funds as well as facilitate direct donations.

Christine Lind Hage, library director and local resident for twenty-five years, took the suggestion to heart and asked to be sponsored for membership in the local Rotary Club. She is now a board member of the Rochester Rotary Club, a stepping-stone to club president, and spends up to a quarter of her job time as a member of several major community groups in town. Besides the Rotary, she is a member of the League of Women Voters and the Chamber of Commerce, among others, and a staff member is dispatched to Lions Club meetings. She also positions herself conspicuously for community events, for example, emceeing the annual community Christmas parade, where she intersperses library chitchat with the required formalities. So dedicated are her community efforts that at a recent function attended by 178 local "movers and shakers," she "knew almost everyone there," and they presumably knew her or, better still, knew the library.

Hage said that her objectives are to make the library more visible as a player in the community. Her strategy seems to be working. In addition to a gift of $3,000 from the Rotary Club for a literacy project and a grant of $15,000 from the Rochester Hills Lions Club to install computers for the visibly impaired, the library is a partner with the Rotary, the City of Rochester Hills, the Downtown Development Authority (DDA), and the Greater Rochester Area Community Foundation (GRACF) to develop a public park on library grounds with perennial gardens, benches, and a gateway entry.

Fund-raising for the $350,000 project is coordinated by the Rotary Club with the GRACF and fourteen local charitable organizations. As described in a written agreement, the Rotary Club is to be responsible for the plantings, the city for construction and snow removal, the DDA for installing and maintaining the lighting and electricity, and the library for cutting and watering the grass. The project, which is scheduled for completion in the summer of 1997, is "directly a result of my community activity," said Hage. Incoming Rochester Rotary Club president Dr. Bill Ebinger agreed that the Rotary's interest in the library was "obviously a result of the librarians' community visibility."

For librarians who seek this route of community advocacy, Hage, president-elect of the Public Library Association, advises, "Get out and talk with community organizations. Bring the library message to groups, but on a one-to-one personal basis. When I'm on a first-name basis with the superintendent of schools, and he comes up like he did on Tuesday at Rotary and says what a great experience he had in our library, I glow! This comment was overheard by another club leader who chirped in that he and his family had a great experience recently [at the library]. This is overheard by others, and goodwill for the library spreads, all because the superintendent of schools felt comfortable coming up to me and making a remark. I figure you can't buy recommendations like that!"

Comment

The library understands that to gain funds, it must be an active player in the community, so it takes the initiative in doing so, touching a variety of bases and forming partnerships. By being in the driver's seat, the library can best control the terms of the partnership so that funding advantage is maximized. As pointed out, the librarian's contacts are a significant factor in partnering, like the "resident schmoozers" at the Prince George's County Memorial Library mentioned in chapter 4. A written agreement that spells out the responsibilities of each party, as mentioned in this partnership, is necessary to help ensure a hassle-free longevity that can benefit future liaisons for funding advantage. The one-to-one relationships that are formed are the "R&D" component of future partnerships.

Chapter 17

Partnering with Community Clout: Reading Public Library, Reading, Pennsylvania

> Programs related to support of universal literacy are of special interest to us because they are closely aligned to our main business focus—that of communication services. The Greater Berks County Book Bonanza project contributes significantly to these objectives by providing financial support to our area libraries and assisting local scholars in furthering their education so that they in turn can serve our community.
>
> —Sandra Keller Williams, postmaster, Reading, Pennsylvania

Library income: $1.8 million
Local government share: 44.5 percent

For over seventeen years, a partnership of the Reading Public Library in Reading, Pennsylvania, has produced an annual book sale known as the Book Bonanza. This project has earned over half a million dollars to benefit the library and its partners.[1] Involving nearly a year of preparation, a team of 300 volunteers, and the sale of a painstakingly selected 75,000 used books and records, this community partnership began when the local AAUW (American Association of University Women) needed more help and asked the library to join its annual book sale effort. Then, the newly organized Friends of the Reading-Berks Public Libraries came aboard, and the three-way partnership fell into place.

Annual revenue for this event held at a shopping mall averages over $37,000, according to Dodson E. Dreisbach, general manager of the Reading sale and founding president of the Friends. Dreisbach said that the sale "transcends its revenue-raising purpose" as an annual community event eagerly anticipated by hundreds of local book lovers.[2] It is a highly organized and carefully planned effort honed over the years by a community-based executive committee of eight that runs a tight ship. For example, they might politely discourage those volunteers—including librarians—who are not in step with the committee's marketing vision. (Librarians are not asked to sort, said a committee member, because "they tend to categorize the books by Dewey decimal and other library methods rather than what will sell.")

A dedicated part of the process is the sorting of some 200,000 community-donated books. Each year, sorting guidelines are reviewed and updated, and pricing is adjusted on the basis of previous years. "We keep in mind changes in taste from one year to the next," said Jackie Brown, who is the chief sorter and the AAUW's representative to the executive committee, "and also the fact that the sale is only three days, which makes our selection criteria different than, say, a used book dealer's. We also consider special local needs, such as class reading lists, and current trends like home schooling." A generous supply of inexpensive general fiction that sells for 25 cents is an important consideration "in order to afford every economic status a chance to buy something." With the better books, on the other hand, attention is paid to market value for competitive pricing. The sorting process is so well controlled that at the end of the sale, less than 3 percent of the books, on average, remain to be hauled away by the recycler. (One year, only three books were left.)

Other considerations (all sales are cash, and checks are not accepted even from members, a policy that irritates book dealers, "but we're not here to service them," said a committee member) and small-cash items are priced at 25 cents, individually or in groups, to reduce the handling of small change.

Thanks to community donations of services, the cost of producing a sale is less than 8 percent of the proceeds, or about $3,000, said Dreisbach. For the cost of $1, the post office rents its basement for the sorting operation, a local trucking company provides three tractor trailers to haul the books to the mall, a container company provides cartons in the dimensions that the committee specifies, and a recycling company picks up the remains.

Most important, 300 volunteers, representing the Friends (membership is 650) and the AAUW, plan, sort, move, sell, and clean up. For a starter, the Reading post office serves as a collection point for books for a week in June. ("It looks like an anthill here," said a postal employee. "People with books running in and out. We gathered 100,000 books in a week.")

From this effort, the Reading Public Library receives about $12,000, or one-third of the total revenue, that might reimburse the "janitorial muscle for book moving" that the library provides, according to Frank Kasprowitz, assistant library director. However, the library also benefits from increased awareness of its existence in the community, which Dreisbach said is the main purpose for which the Friends group is organized. With this in mind, the Friends applied their third of the revenue in 1995 to producing a publicity video on the library, with Edwin Newman of NBC fame volunteering as narrator. (He was recruited by a colleague.)

The video is distributed to schools, community groups, and local legislators who, it is hoped, will respond where it counts. The newsletter—a sixteen-page bimonthly—is also distributed to local legislators and mayors of the various municipalities, the superintendent of schools, and the Chamber of Commerce. The cost of producing the video was $6,500, and the yearly budget for the journal is $7,500. The final third of the book sale revenue is distributed among the nineteen other libraries in the Berks County system.

Other benefits to the community, reported by Dreisbach, are that "sales in bookstores in the mall soar during Book Bonanza. Also, the literacy council, which has a sign-up table during the sale, enlists dozens of volunteers to help teach others to read." Therefore, thanks to the library's Friends, the city of Reading's name lives into perpetuity—or at least in writing, for the spoken version is pronounced "redding."

Comment

Library Friends and other volunteers are often the real "bonanza" behind library funding efforts. The Reading library partnership is a relatively long one in library circles for which its dedicated volunteers can be credited. The Friends group, started for cultural activities such as book and author lunches, now looks to extending its efforts in the political arena to secure the local funding that has long evaded Pennsylvania's municipalities.

As the AAUW initiated the book fair and, appropriately, saw the library as a valuable partner, so do other organizations seek library partnerships. To their benefit, libraries are now taking the initiatives themselves and finding their own partners for funding advantage, as this chapter illustrates.

The book sale reveals characteristics of a successful partnership: the attention to project planning, the control of costs, and incorporating other community entities, in this case, volunteers, small businesses, and the local post office. The partnering Friends also keep their library support current through the newsletter and video, both of which serve as tools in the political advocacy envisioned. Finally, the book sale itself provides a foundation for additional library public relations, perhaps including displays featuring various library programs, a video corner spotlighting the library, and a local political figure presenting a library award at peak time during the event.

Notes

1. "Book Bonanza Reach for Half-a-Million Was Close but . . . ," *Bookends, Journal of the Friends of Reading-Berks Public Libraries,* vol. 14, no. 5 (September/October 1996), p. 3.

2. "Bonanza Had Modest Start . . . ," *Bookends, Journal of the Friends of Reading-Berks Public Libraries,* vol. 13, no. 4 (July/August 1995), p. 5.

Chapter 18

Partnering with Community Clout: St. Paul Public Library, St. Paul, Minnesota

> I think by now, they all feel they're good enough to play in the big leagues.
>
> —Gene Lamont, manager of the Pittsburgh Pirates baseball team,
> quoted in Robert Dvorchak, "Pirates Fans . . . ",
> *Pittsburgh Post-Gazette,* October 21, 1997, special section, p. 5

Library income: $9.7 million
Local government share: 90 percent

A promising partnership of the Friends of the St. Paul Public Library, launched in 1997, is currently in the initial stage after nearly a year of planning. Its purpose is to enable four of the largest nonprofit small business assistance providers in the Twin Cities area to remotely access pertinent online business reference materials as well as some of one another's resources, such as templates and formats for business plans. In this way, the library can indirectly extend library services to new business users who are its partners' clients. It also expands services directly to its own business users as new materials are purchased in fulfillment of the partnership's terms and by access to its partners' unique resources and counseling services.

The $200,000, three-year funded alliance was initiated by its funder—the Norwest Foundation of Norwest Corporation—after the library expressed its interest in helping the city's developing minority businesses. "We're interested in working with partners of color and of low income, which describes the current users of the library's business resources. We're not interested in targeting major corporations. The library's role is in outreach to the underserved community," said Peter D. Pearson, executive director of the Friends of the St. Paul

Public Library, in which role he is also a member of the library's administrative staff responsible for program development.

The four project partners, which are both publicly and privately funded, are WomenVenture, which specializes in providing minority and low-income women with the skills needed for economic self-sufficiency; the Metropolitan Economic Development Association (MEDA), which provides assistance to businesses owned and managed by ethnic residents of Minnesota; the Neighborhood Development Center (NDC), which helps emerging low-income and minority entrepreneurs develop successful businesses that serve inner-city communities; and the Small Business Development Center at the University of St. Thomas, which provides consulting, training, and information resources to entrepreneurs. According to the project proposal, these small business assistance programs have created hundreds of new jobs and businesses in the Twin Cities area, where WomenVenture alone serves more than 3,000 clients per year, helping them find jobs, plan careers, and start and develop businesses.[1]

The library Friends, a 501.c.3. organization has orchestrated the partnership and serves as the fiscal and managing agent. It is a "full-service" organization that has five employees (three are full time), funding from a $7 million endowment, and the authority usually held by a library foundation to raise funds both publicly and privately. The partners, who met for nearly a year to build relationships, familiarize themselves with one another's programs, and decide how to proceed, have their own reasons for partnering. According to Warren McLean, president and chief executive officer of MEDA, the fact that the venture will enable his organization to tap into the library's resources without going to the library is akin to shopping from home. By saving clients time, it will increase their incentive to consume or, in this case, to do research, he said.

Kay Gudmestad, executive director of WomenVenture, said that partnering with the library provides "credibility" for her organization. "The library's funding base is broader than ours. They bring to the table the advantages of size and capability," she said. WomenVenture's clients are already challenged by changes, such as the transition from welfare to work and English as a second language, said Gudmestad, so staff must accompany them to the library—often a new and unfamiliar place—to obtain the materials that will now be available online. The library affiliation will "save us time; we can take them to a bank instead," said Gudmestad.

How do the costs of the project stack up? According to the project's written proposal, funding is for three years, during which time the library will install dedicated computer workstations at each of the four business assistance centers and at the library and one of its branches. Branch users especially fit well with the project's focus, as 33 percent of residents are below the poverty level, and over 11 percent were unemployed, according to the 1990 census.

Online and equipment costs will be assumed by each of the partners. The library estimates its phone charges at $500 per month. The additional costs do not seem to be an issue for the partners. "We save man-hours in time," said McLean. "That's an overall cost benefit." In addition, he figures that by using the library's free resources, they might be able to replace the "expensive" on-line technical service that they are currently using. "This brings us additional resources. The time we've taken in building relationships will ultimately be worth it," said Gudmestad. Costs of a half-time project coordinator who will train partners in equipment use and other aspects of the project are covered by the initial grant. After that, the job is expected to be phased out, although Pearson said this might change.

The advantage to funding in the long term is that the project adds to the library's portfolio of social services to low-income and minority individuals. Private funders are looking to fund programs that are "not business-as-usual," said Pearson, "especially programs to the disadvantaged and poor. Having this stronger constituency at the library can help." As for public funders, they like the possibility of helping entrepreneurs who might increase the city's tax base, said Pearson.

Comment

This partnership is a creative arrangement that, in addition to the library, consolidates and expands services for four community-based organizations. By extending the library's influence in the city's economic and low-income areas, the library is hitting two targets of local and national funding emphasis, and this should increase its community power base in future funding negotiations. The plans are a model in successful partnering: the project is library initiated and directed; attention is given to laying the groundwork well in advance; the missions of the five organizations are congruent with the library's mission; the partners bring new constituents to the library; the project brings new materials and services for the library's clients; partners seem to have good reasons to stay tied into the arrangement; partners share the costs; and costs, for which funding is secure for three years, are figured to decline, so the library could cover the costs out of its operating funds. This is a project from which the library would seem to gain much and risk little. To complete the arrangements, a signed written agreement and an escape plan for the library should be included.

Note

1. Project proposal and letter from Peter D. Pearson to Norwest Corporation, September 3, 1996, unpublished, 2 pp.

Chapter 19

Partnering with Local Business Clout: Brooklyn Public Library's Business Library, Brooklyn, New York

> Apart from the fact that no business could open its doors if there were no language, culture, data, information and know-how, there is the deeper fact that of all the resources needed to create wealth, none is more versatile than knowledge.
>
> — Alvin and Heidi Toffler, *The Politics of the Third Wave* (Atlanta: Turner Publishing, 1995), p. 37

Library materials income: $525,000

A short-term partnership to benefit local business was implemented recently by the Brooklyn Public Library's Business Library (BPLBL) and the Consolidated Edison Company of New York (Con Ed), supplier of electric and gas utilities to the New York City area. The business library, dating back to 1943, has been a venerable resource to small business in the New York City area and in far-reaching corners of the state and the world. In fact, New York State recently installed an 800 number for state businesses to access the library. In 1996, the library chalked up reader statistics of 83,000 reference contacts.

The opening in 1996 in the same city (but different borough) of the much-publicized New York Public Library's Science, Business and Industry Library (SIBIL) had some impact at first in lowering use at the BPLBL, according to Joan Canning, library director, as library users hurried over to check out "the new kid on the block." However, the BPLBL's niche in personal services, open stacks, and an archive of older references are not easily outdone by an upstart. Add to this a burgeoning interest in partnering, and the portfolio grows.

The Con Ed partnership was initiated by the company, following a history of library largess that started with a fax machine to facilitate the "enormous number of phone requests" they get, said Stewart Leffler, Con Ed's manager of economic development. The partnership involved a grant of $20,000 from Con Ed, a portion of which was used to present three breakfast programs that featured speakers on topics of interest to local businesses. "Through the library, we can reach small business. They are an ally and very visible in downtown Brooklyn," said Leffler. The mission of Con Ed's economic development program is to assist local businesses with expansion plans, to attract new companies to the area, and to retain the ones already there, according to Leffler.

The library made the arrangements for the programs, which were held in its 100-seat auditorium; publicized the events to its users and to lists provided by Con Ed; capitalized on the occasion by distributing literature on its services to the 300 attendees; and provided "quick tours," according to a publicity brochure.

"The library realizes its potential in this kind of arrangement," said Elisa Glenn, the library's newly appointed outreach specialist. "Many companies would like a neutral resource to reach their audiences. Our audience is very targeted for them."

The library staff also connects with the local business community through Chamber of Commerce membership on the small business committee. "Librarians need to go out and develop relationships," said Leffler. "Library staff are a part of the business community, there are business teams out there. . . . Librarians can't sit in the office."

Comment

This is an example of a mutually beneficial community partnership that positions the library favorably for future partnerships and future funding. Business partnerships are increasing in number among public libraries but still rank far behind partnerships with nonprofits, such as schools. However, business partnerships can be highly useful for all concerned. Businesses use the library and donate dollars to community organizations, their staff sit on library governing boards, and they want contact for marketing purposes with library customers (the most prominent illustration of this being Microsoft Corporation's partnership, outlined in chapter 20). Con Ed has clout as an important business entity in the library's service area, and the reputation gained from implementing a partnering project with the company would carry weight for the library's future partnerships. Con Ed's audience (local small businesses) and its educational objectives in the partnership are also consistent with the library's. With the addition of a community outreach specialist, the library is prepared to initiate its own library-directed partnerships now that it has its feet wet.

Chapter 20

Partnering with Big-Business Clout: Libraries Online!

> High tech companies are increasingly alarmed about a dearth of skilled employees, and helping to bring technology to schools and libraries is a concrete way to help the underprivileged. Of course, the two efforts [by Microsoft and Oracle Corporations] also serve to familiarize people who could become customers with Microsoft software and Oracle's network computers, an added benefit to both companies.
>
> —"Software Moguls Suddenly Compete to Be Nice Guys,"
> *Wall Street Journal,* June 25, 1997, p. A3

> The Gates' gift . . . serves as a catalyst for libraries to attract funding at the local level. The libraries of America will benefit greatly. . . . They will double that benefit if the Gates' generosity convinces others to invest in libraries.
>
> —Walter Hansen, "The Fund for America's Libraries," memo,
> American Library Association, July 17, 1997

Following a pilot project in 1995 in which nine U.S. library systems were awarded $4 million in funding, training, and software, the American Library Association (ALA) entered into a one-year partnership with Microsoft Corporation for the Libraries Online! (LOL) project. For the ALA, this partnership meant that some forty-one U.S. library systems would be recipients of an additional $10.5 million in awards to enable public online access, especially to those who would not otherwise have it. Microsoft, which initiated the venture, would expect to benefit in several ways from the project's stated objective— "to research and develop innovative approaches for extending information technologies to underserved communities" and would also have use of the ALA's prestigious name.[1]

The public visibility of the ALA's partner, with chairman Bill Gates especially active in the project, carries significant weight in helping libraries leverage local funding from their LOL donations. The Microsoft grant has been "a wonderful vehicle for leveraging funding," according to Lynn Wheeler, assistant director of the Baltimore County Public Library (income $22.3 million) in Towson, Maryland. The first year of the project, the library was scheduled for a $300,000 reduction in funding, but just prior to the budget preparation by the county executive, the library's LOL site opened with local politicians present, said Wheeler. When the budget was announced, the "mark had been restored, plus $30,000. When we asked for additional computer replacement funds so that we could make use of the Microsoft products the company gave us, we got an additional $200,000 above our budget."

At the Phoenix Public Library (income $17.4 million) in Phoenix, Arizona, library director Toni Garvey said that the city council is "astounded" by the increased use of the library with public online access—which she thinks could help future funding. In addition, the LOL funding resulted in donations of Internet training sessions for staff and public by Executrain, a company that specializes in corporate employee training. According to librarian Merrilyn Ridgeway, the company agreed to reserve "300 slots" for library staff training sessions over the next two years at its Phoenix facility, hold public training sessions quarterly at the library, and provide the library with two sets of its CD-ROM training programs. Benefits to the company, according to general manager James Young, are that employees have a greater sense of their own worth for the work that they do in the community; in addition, the more people who are literate in the computer world, the more potential clients for his company that trains corporate employees in the United States and other parts of the world in the use of computer software and other technical processes.

At the Martin Library (income $1.4 million) in York, Pennsylvania, Mark Merrifield, director of operations, said that the grant has made it possible for the library to leverage an endowment from the local township that they have had their eye on but were unable to secure until they came up with the idea of a new electronic library replicating the one made possible by the LOL grant at the library's main facility. The new lab will be located in a new building at a private graphic arts school with which the library—in its entrepreneurial mode—has had a long-standing contract for library services. Impressed with the project and the speed with which the library has gotten it all together—four months for the main installation and a couple months or less for the replication—Microsoft has agreed to donate the software for the new lab, estimated at over $40,000. In addition to the endowment, other funding for the replication is from the township and the school, which will house the new library, according to a memo of agreement that is renewable annually, said Merrifield.

A "three-way leverage" at the Central Arkansas Library System (income $4.8 million) in Little Rock, Arkansas—a result of the library's interest in bringing together books with automated resources—allows the library to get into the underserved areas that libraries often ignore because of insufficient funds, said library director Bobby Roberts. The library came up with the idea of a bookmobile service to community centers and housing projects in underserved areas that, in addition to transporting several hundred books, provides four computers with public Internet access. Using the fact of the Microsoft dollars, said Roberts, the library was able to get $60,000 in capital funding from the federal Housing and Urban Development (HUD) office and then, with both these grants in hand, approached the Rockefeller Trust, which provided an additional $50,000 in capital funds for a total $138,000.

The library system provides about $18,000 in operational costs for the bookmobile, such as gasoline and the drivers, and HUD and the local community centers pay for the communication lines. Two more leveraging acts came about when using the Microsoft grant. First, the library approached a local foundation—the Roy and Christine Sturgis Charitable and Educational Trust—to fund the computer lab in its new downtown location, and then, as a result of the Sturgis grant, Microsoft contributed software to the project.

At the Elizabeth Public Library (income $2.9 million) in Elizabeth, New Jersey, library director Joseph J. Keenan said that the library leveraged LOL funds for $25,000 in local funds from the James C. Kellogg Foundation and $2,500 from Exxon Corporation to pay for new workstations in the lab and to make a contribution to a new facility for children. The fact that the library was awarded the grant had a positive impact on the library's application for the local grants, said Keenan. Capitalizing on the opening of its Internet laboratory, the library held a ceremony that included the mayor, a congressman, and donors and that was widely covered by the local print media.

Louise Blalock, director of the Hartford Public Library (income $5.1 million) in Hartford, Connecticut, said that "hard cash is not the main issue; what is most important is what we're able to deliver" in particular, as the library has a combination public library and elementary school—we want to show publicly "what we can do for kids." The Microsoft funds brought "new capabilities we hadn't had before, which also helped us get funds for more PCs in the branch libraries."

After receiving $20,000 in local county funds for space renovation following its LOL grant, the Wicomico County Free Library (income $1.2 million) in Salisbury, Maryland, publicized its computer labs with a five-color logo donated by a local graphic artist and the trademark WILL, for Wicomico Information and Learning Library. "It helps sell the concept as something new and different," said library director Kathleen Reif, "and implies that this is a very natural and legitimate role for the public library. . . . It works here," she said, noting that one member of the county council said that he wanted "a WILL site in his neighborhood." He never would have asked for "a library," she said.

Another reason for success in leveraging the LOL grants is that "it helps to have Bill Gates on your side; people know who he is," said Roberts.

Comment

This partnership is probably the best illustration of what leveraging can do when the right ingredients are in place, especially those of munificence and partner's clout. The leveraging examples offer possibilities that are as varied as the libraries and communities that are involved. They emphasize several principles of effective library funding advocacy: the importance of who your partner is, the novelty of your project and how well it is managed, the good public service that results, the numbers of users and who those users are, the other agencies that have contributed to the funding, and having local politicians present at prestigious openings.

The details of this partnership might be useful information for helping public libraries put together their own local partnerships. However, the ALA chooses not to reveal the details of the process or the exact terms of the partnership. One high-ranking librarian indicated that controversy exists in the profession over various aspects of the partnership, some feeling that the ALA might have sold out. The lesson for public libraries is that local partnerships make sense only when they are consistent with the values of the local environment and the library involved. "Just because a potential partner is there does not necessarily mean it should be partnered with," said the librarian interviewed.

Note

1. *Libraries Online!*, project summary, 1996.

Chapter 21

Conclusion

> Managers of nonprofits must ask themselves the following: Do we have clout with certain groups of people? Some nonprofit organizations can help corporations gain access to people who influence consumers' purchases.
>
> — Alan R. Andreason, "Profits for Nonprofits:
> Find a Corporate Partner," *Harvard Business Review,*
> November–December 1996, pp. 56, 57

The foregoing accounts of successful library partnerships describe a number of characteristics of these partnerships in current library practice that work to funding advantage. These are identified as follows.

The Library

- The library initiates the partnership through its community outreach.
- The library recognizes its own strengths and how these could be desirable to its partner; it also negotiates with the partner from a position of strength.
- The library is aware of, and is not in disagreement with, the partner's ethical standards.
- Preliminary to the partnership agreement, a dedicated effort is made to become acquainted with the partner, its institutional mission, its objectives in the proposed partnership, and the specific resources that it is prepared to bring to the partnership.
- The library knows what the partner can and cannot do for the project.

The Partner(s)

- The partner has business, social, and/or political ties to the community.
- The partner has a good track record in community partnerships.
- The partner is sophisticated in the area of operation that the library expects it to contribute to.
- The partner's and the library's clientele are congruous.
- The partner brings different and unique viewpoints that facilitate the partnership's goals.
- The partner values the library for reasons that the library wants to be valued.

Funding

- The partnership is expected to generate funds for the library or to position the library favorably for funding whether or not this is the partnership's main objective.
- Funds or other benefits as an outcome of the partnership are leveraged into funds, materials, publicity, and/or other advantages for the library.

Goals

- The partners agree on the goals of the partnership.
- The goals of the partnership fit with the missions of the library and its partner(s).
- The process for achieving the goals is initiated and controlled by the partners in a well-planned and dedicated effort.
- The suitability of the partnership's goals for its intended audience has been verified by the partners.

Process and Outcomes

- The partners agree not only to the goals of the partnership but also to the process for accomplishing those goals.
- The partners sign a written agreement.
- The partners together initiate and control the process in a dedicated effort.
- The process of achieving the goals utilizes the resources of other community organizations or individuals in the community.
- The partnership's goals are reviewed by partners and administrators on a regularly determined basis.

- The partnership has the continuing support of the administration and governing boards of all the partnering organizations.
- Those who are intended to benefit from the partnership's objective are periodically informed about this objective.
- The partnership generates ideas for future library partnerships.
- The partnership has secondary outcomes that also facilitate the library's mission.

RULE 4

TALK ASSETS
(LIBRARY RESOURCES FOR
FUNDING ADVANTAGE)

Chapter 22

Introduction

> Assets—the value of tangible things, such as cash and inventory, and that of intangibles, such as a trademark or goodwill.
>
> —*The Heritage Illustrated Dictionary of the English Language*

> Adding value to the lives of citizens is really what community assets are about. They can take many forms and shapes—a library, a zoo, a park, a symphony, a stadium—because we are a diverse people with many interests. All of them add value by allowing us to learn, share, and to recreate together.
>
> —David Matter, chairman, Allegheny Regional Asset District, Pittsburgh, Pennsylvania

Certain library assets, when effectively managed, are especially prized by community residents and serve as rallying points for library funding advocacy. They include tangibles (e.g., books, computer workstations, and special collections) and an intangible: quality public service. Libraries define their assets for purposes of planning and management by looking at what might be called indicators of community interest and shareholding. These indicators are comments from the public, community opinion polls, statements from elected officials, what funders will fund, the numbers of users, government initiatives, media emphases, and the experiences of other libraries. Most important, once libraries clarify their community assets (e.g., as they might do in creating mission statements and long-range plans), it is necessary to manage these assets for funding advantage. This includes providing ample publicity to those library users who might benefit from knowing that the asset exists as well as alerting public funders who are in a position to benefit the library's funding.

Public libraries can be marketed as quality-of-life enhancers. Mall and residential developers recognize their marketing advantage when they look to incorporate public libraries in new development projects. Elected officials also count on the magnetic draw of public libraries. Commenting on his constituents collecting 25,000 signatures to build a new library in his Chicago neighborhood, Alderman Eugene Schulter said, "It really boils down to quality of life; libraries mean a center of activity, bringing people for concerts, readings, lectures." Libraries also have a role in economic and social leveling when certain advantages might not otherwise be possible. For example, libraries provide employment information for job seekers, assist the competitive advantage of small-business owners, and create jobs and community economic opportunities by their very existence as facilities that need constructing, renovation, human resources, and other essentials. These are the particulars that prompt advocates to "talk assets."

Using the following guide, the following chapters describe how selected assets work for library funding advantage in several current situations. Characteristics of these assets are introduced as follows:

- The asset generates local funding or favorably positions the library for local funding.
- The library recognizes the asset as a community asset.
- The asset supports the library's mission.
- The asset is subject to specific policies and procedures and is administered by trained staff.
- The asset has the continued support of library management and the board of directors.
- The asset responds to a community need and is flexible in its structure to reflect changes in community needs.
- The asset demonstrates special and unique service to its users.
- The asset is publicized regularly to users and to public and private funders.

The conclusion in chapter 28 extends these guidelines on the basis of information in the following field accounts.

Chapter 23

Federal Dollars for Local Business: Toledo-Lucas County Public Library, Toledo, Ohio

These days, rather than trying to lure giant corporations from else-where, Ohio is more likely to use its development dollars to nurture its own small and midsize businesses.

—Paulette Thomas, "Ohio Nurtures Homegrown Companies,"
Wall Street Journal, March 31, 1997, p. A2

For people starting a business we direct them to the library. Its Government Procurement Center (GPC) uses minimum contract dollars to leverage hundreds more. Even with a decrease in GPC funds, there is no obvious dip in their service. They are there to help—especially small businesses that do not have the resources of the large ones.

—Wendy Gramza, Toledo Area Chamber of Commerce, July 1997

Library budget: $20.2 million
Local government share: 24 percent

While saving small and midsize businesses extensive costs in dollars and time, the Government Procurement Center (GPC) of the Toledo-Lucas County Public Library in Toledo, Ohio, is also helping companies haul in millions of contract dollars. Its mission, according to center administrator Galen Avery, is to increase the number of federal contract dollars going to small and midsize businesses in the library's sixteen-county service area. Referred to as a "force multiplier," it leverages income to multiply jobs and the tax base of its service area. In 1996, it serviced over 230 customers, of whom 117 received $39 million in federal civilian and military contract awards—or a possible gain in income tax revenues for the library's service area of nearly $10 million, according to Avery. Another formula used for the same figures, known as a "modified RIMS II—Regional Input Modeling System," estimates nearly $72 million in economic impact.

The GPC started in 1983 when the Toledo Area Chamber of Commerce was approached by local businesses to solve the problem of the thirteen- to twenty-four-week delays in receiving the solicitation packages they needed to bid on federal contracts. The Chamber considered the problem for several weeks before reaching the conclusion that the solution was in the library's domain. According to Margaret Danziger, the library's assistant director, the library, whose business department is its "busiest" department, was glad to get the job. The economic hardships of the 1980s were curtailing local businesses, and the center was able to facilitate the process of bringing in federal contracts. "We see it as a local government assistance program," said Danziger, adding that the numbers served are "far undercounted" because many clients do not reply to questionnaires.

Originally concerned with document retrieval, the service gradually extended its efforts to provide online access to locating bids, computer-generated specifications and standards in two hours where it previously took a day (and before that, several weeks) for microform-based data, and a significant research and counseling component for companies just entering the government contracting arena and for those that are already there.

The GPC is a "full-service shop," said Avery. Counseling, which was started to help customers interpret information in the documents and to decipher "legalese," now includes more sophisticated "high-tech problems," competitive intelligence, other "tips and guideposts," and alternative dispute resolutions that can save $200,000 in litigation fees.

An overview of the industries served by the center indicates that about 40 percent are in manufacturing (everything from office furniture to cruise missiles, said Avery), construction, and the service sector (especially in architectural engineering and the software industry). Research for these companies can involve, among other things, finding sources of supply. For example, a company manufacturing ice melters landed a $1 million contract after the center prepared a list of suppliers of the better and cheaper materials they wanted. Another company that manufactures fake missiles (Why have a $2 million product when a $200,000 one will do? asked Avery) requested research on camouflage patterns and other military deception technology that the federal government had collected, and a missile manufacturer required research going back twenty years that resulted in a 150-page report by Avery and staff.

The fact that the library is a government depository of print materials on a variety of subjects, from aviation to military, and also has access to numerous databases enables the center to fill research needs at no cost to the customer for time and labor, thus saving small companies huge amounts of money. According to Avery, to his knowledge the center is the only one in the country that is based in a public library; others are at regional economic development centers, chambers of commerce, and university sites. A spokesman at an equivalent service provider in southwestern Pennsylvania that is part of a government regional development council and without a separate budget said that his service provides only technical support for clients. When clients need government information, they must order subscriptions to the government publications that the Toledo-Lucas library already receives as part of its depository status.

Helen Dennis, whose six-and-a-half-year old relocation services company, the Project Advantage Group in Toledo, has gained $4 million in government contracts. She said that before using the GPC services, it took a year on the phone to get contacts and inside information, make contract arrangements, get procurement regulations, and deal with the various issues of government. Now, Dennis says, the GPC is "my guide, interpreter, and translator to help me understand this world and where to start, which can be mind-boggling." In addition to pinpointing and fine-tuning the information necessary for the procurement process, the GPC, which is hooked up to the Commerce Business Daily (CBD), e-mails (previously faxed) the information that is relevant to her category of business. "The service is a vital part of this area's economic development," said Dennis.

The GPC's current budget is $170,000, of which 60 percent is from the library's operating budget, 8 percent from the State of Ohio, and 32 percent from the federal government's Defense Logistics Agency under a statewide contract for all procurement centers. Since 1990, the GPC has averaged over $31 million annually in contracts.[1] Avery regularly toots the GPC's horn in talks to the Rotary Club, the Chamber of Commerce, and other community organizations. "The GPC's services overturn some of the public's assumptions about the library," he said. "For some of our clients, it's the first time since high school they've set foot in a library, and they become converted library users and fans."

Comment

The State of Ohio gives special emphasis to small businesses (those with 500 employees or fewer), which account for 86 percent of its companies and employ nearly half its workers.[2] Given this incentive on the part of the state government, which funds the major portion of the library's budget, the GPC is facilitating the objectives of local government as well as easing a dilemma of its local chamber of commerce.

The GPC's high usage reinforces its role as a community asset. In addition, its structure is flexible so that it can expand services as it sees fit to best respond to its users. It also performs unique services not typical of other library services (e.g., a 150-page research report without charge to clients), demonstrating its dedicated commitment to public service. It recognizes the critical nature of its service, and this has a direct bearing on the balance sheets of the companies it serves, as confirmed by one of its clients. Service providers also make a point of publicizing the program so that all who might benefit from it know of its existence. Finally, the service is said to benefit the library by increasing general collection usage.

The GPC is an asset that requires constant attention to keep abreast both of knowledge that is pertinent to new industries and of government incentives. Because employee training is an area of importance to the state for which it subcontracts to outside organizations, the library, with its client base, print and online resources, and meeting space, could be an ideal subcontractor, enhancing its value even more.

Notes

1. Faxed memo from Avery, with GPC chart and graph, April 1997.
2. Paulette Thomas, "Ohio Nurtures Homegrown Companies," *Wall Street Journal,* March 31, 1997, p. A2.

Chapter 24

Museum-Quality Fine Art Collection: Kokomo-Howard County Public Library, Kokomo, Indiana

The collection adds some substance to the library aside from books. It's spread out throughout all the library, not just locked up in a room somewhere, but part of the actual decor. . . . In our work, we field calls for people coming from all over for meetings. The art is an added attraction in a town this small where there's no Disneyland.

—Peggy Hudson, director,
Kokomo-Howard County Visitors Bureau

Library income: $2.8 million
Local government share: 86 percent

On the outside of the building of the Kokomo-Howard County Public Library in Kokomo, Indiana, is the inscription "Community Center for Culture and Information," which only hints at the unique collection of fine art within. No other U.S. public libraries are known to have an actively growing museum-quality fine art collection such as the 120-piece Hoosier Art Collection at Kokomo.

Started in the early 1900s, the collection of Indiana artists' work was expanded in the 1960s by director Philip T. Hamilton and then by Hamilton's successor and current library director, Charles N. Joray.[1] The collection fits the library's mission to educate and provide recreation for the community, said Joray, and it also fills a niche as one of the few public art collections in the city and the only one with the particular focus of nineteenth- and twentieth-century Hoosier painting and fine prints. It includes award-winning Indiana artists exhibited in the annual Hoosier Salon—a juried show of contemporary artists, such as Leota Williams Loop, Theodore Clement Steele, Clifton Wheeler, and five works of internationally known artist Misch Kohn.[2]

"It's a wonderful thing for the library to have not only books, tapes, and all the other resources but to be able to expose clients to high-quality art from Indiana," said Michael Byron, Indianapolis art dealer in historical Indiana paintings who has done occasional business with the library. "Kokomo is part of a very active art market interested in its heritage. We applaud what's being done as part of the mission to provide a lot of experiences for their clients."

Joray, who is a musician but had not been an art aficionado, got interested in the art "under pressure" when someone who was hired as an art cataloger under a $5,000 grant quit in the middle of the project. At the time, Joray was vacationing in Brown County, Indiana—a mecca for Indiana artists. He found a book on Hoosier art written for fourth-graders, studied it, and came back and finished the catalog, fulfilling the terms of the grant. In the process, he educated himself about Hoosier art and trained his eye. "The bug bites you," he said. Whenever he has extra time, he works with the art collection and enjoys negotiating with art dealers and auctioneers and "the bickering that is part of the process."

One or two paintings, averaging in the $3,000 to $5,000 price range, are added annually. These are funded by the library's gift and memorial funds, which accumulate some $250 a month from a continual sale of used books located at the library's circulation desk (hardbacks 50 cents, softcovers 25 cents). Maintaining the collection, including conservation, restoration, and framing, is less than half a percent of the library's operating budget—about $10,000, according to graphic artist and collection curator James W. Hoover. In 1997, an appraisal of the collection for insurance purposes, at a cost of $2,500, was approved by the library's seven-member board of trustees (appointed by local county and school board officials). A previous appraisal in the late 1980s in which the collection was valued at $1 million is expected to be substantially increased.

The collection is exhibited six to eight times per year in one of the monthly art exhibitions in the library's exhibit area stretching along 270 linear feet of wide hallways near the children's collection and the public meeting rooms— areas of high visibility, according to Hoover.

In addition to buying work from the Hoosier Salon, Joray tracks down items that come to his attention from dealers and collectors, taking with him an art-knowledgeable person. The library's "Art Collection Policy" of 1989 (see item 2 in appendix 2) spells out the terms of selection, specifically that "prior to a decision to purchase a work of art, at least two knowledgeable people will have been asked to comment on it. . . . Also, an opinion concerning the value of the work of art will be obtained from at least one reputable source other than the seller." Joray said that to simplify matters, it was decided that only pieces over $2,000 needed approval by the board of trustees before purchase.

The collection receives public exposure not only from the more than 250,000 visitors to the main building annually but also through occasional loans to local museums for exhibitions and for the reproduction of various pieces in art publications. In addition, a twenty-five-page full-color catalog is distributed, and a scholarly fifty-page large-size softcover book on artist Leota Williams Loop (written by Hoover and published in 1996) is sold in a Brown County art gallery. The book—a $20,000 project, including staff time—was funded by the library Friends, the state art commission, local businesses, and a windfall the library received when its cooperative circulation system was dissolved and returned the library's investment, said Joray. When the collection is not on exhibit, it is kept in a readily accessible storage area that is available by appointment to scholars and other interested visitors.

According to Joray, the Kokomo economy is "good"—unemployment is low, factories are expanding, and much new construction is being done. Increasing property values allow stable and growing library funding through a library tax district, enabling the art collection as well to grow as it aims to include 200 pieces. Former library board member Xenia Cord said that during her tenure on the board in the early 1990s, the collection had been "refined in its direction," and pieces not appropriate were deaccessioned. One of the collection's strong points, she noted, was the number of female artists represented. The board at that time considered the art collection "a tremendous asset and the best public collection of Hoosier art in the state."

Comment

The library's asset is a product of the community's historical and artistic output. By attempting to enhance its asset (i.e., periodic review so that acquisitions fill historical and aesthetic gaps, distribution of scholarly catalogs, professional appraisals, and other curatorial procedures), the library provides the local community with an asset that links it to the world at large beyond its geographical location and that provides a local cultural resource. As the art dealer, Michael Byron said, "People who walk in may not know exactly what they're looking at, but they know it is original art, and as time goes on it sticks in the back of their minds—they hear the artists' names again and again."

A possibility for further leveraging of this asset to bring more visibility to the library and community is to circulate the pieces for exhibition at other libraries, public galleries, and museums rather than storing them when they are not on display. Attention gained outside the local community could stimulate local attention, including that from library funding agents. The fact that libraries have recently become linked with the museum world on the federal level through the restructured Institute of Museum and Library Services might increase the likelihood of grant money for art collection projects of various kinds.

Notes

1. Leonard B. Pelkey, *Books Along the Wildcat: History of the Kokomo-Howard County Public Library* (Kokomo, Ind.: The Library, 1990), p. 296.

2. James W. Hoover and Heather Dale, *Hoosier Art Collection of the Kokomo-Howard County Public Library* (Kokomo, Ind.: The Library, 1989).

Chapter 25

Government Educational Initiatives: Tucson-Pima Library, Tucson, Arizona

> Many times cities will ignore the activities of the mind. It's much easier to put up a basketball hoop than to develop a meaningful program that can truly impact a child's life.
>
> —Molly McKasson, Tucson City Council member,
> in a letter to the author, August 6, 1997

Library income: $13.4 million
Local government share: 99 percent

Like many urban libraries, the Tucson-Pima Library (TPPL) in Tucson, Arizona, is involved in the business of educating children—providing reading and homework skills that traditionally have been the sole responsibility of public schools or families. However, because of the way in which various social issues play out, the library, along with other community organizations, has stepped in to assume the role of educator. Programs at TPPL that address this role are a family literacy program called Burgers and Books, an after-school program called Homework Help, and another program that encourages teenage parents to read aloud to their children.

The programs are operated in conjunction with the Citizen and Neighborhood Services (CNS) initiative of the City of Tucson, which has set up what it refers to as "neighborhood enhancement teams " (NETeams), which help local neighborhoods respond to needs of residents by the combined efforts of public and private interests. As one of the city departments involved in CNS, the library participates in the NETeams projects when appropriate.[1] All these programs position the library for "good continued support from city tax funds," said Agnes Griffin, library director.

Burgers and Books was started in 1995 by a community youth organization in Tucson known as the Pima Youth Organization (PYO), whose mission is to increase literacy and family reading, preferably working in partnerships, according to Luan E. Wagner, executive director. Someone in the organization observed that library use was infrequent in the rural northwest part of Pima County—a county nearly twice the size of the state of Connecticut—although the library's bookmobile operated there. Armed with this piece of information and the idea of food—"If there is food, they will come," claimed the program's originator—the PYO approached the library and the local McDonald's to partner in a program that would involve families in reading and food, in that order. "It fit with our goal to support literacy," said Laura Thomas Sullivan, the library's outreach director. In an eight-month period, the library increased its bookmobile services to twice monthly and relocated to stops such as elementary school cafeterias that had space to accommodate the activity.

According to a city project report, the initial response to the program was "staggering": 120 persons at one elementary school on opening night and 140 at the second session.[2] At least 700 people currently participate, said Wagner. The library provides the reading materials, responds to special requests, and arranges entertainment (e.g., a magic show). Books and burgers are delivered, and neighborhood teens get part-time jobs helping with the arrangements.

Funded piecemeal by the Community Partnership of Southern Arizona (CPSA) and the various sites where the program is located, Wagner said that the PYO has to write many requests for proposals to fund all twelve sites, as it is responsible for securing project funding. Costs range from $3,000 to $5,000 per site per year for a site with 65 to 200 attendees. The food portion is the major cost, sometimes requiring a drive of thirty-five miles or more for the burgers.

Besides Burgers and Books, the library is involved in the Homework Help homework assistance program, with thirty centers at library branches, Boys and Girls Clubs, and a mall, all of which the library stocks with reference materials and tutors. The program was started with a grant provided by local antiracketeering funds that the city made available to community nonprofits, according to Sullivan, and is now funded by the library's operating funds.

According to Sullivan, because these programs fit with the library's goals, they work. It is her "dream" that the schools will someday be able to do Homework Help. Until then, however, the library's effort "demonstrates clearly to all that we are not just recreational, we are an educational institution."

The library is facilitating the funding for these programs, which are recognized as vital to high school graduates, preparing them for education at the community colleges and in the job market. "We can contribute to that—we are one of the few organizations in the community that can," said Sullivan. "We are open long hours when people who work and go to school part time need the library. The library is critical to economic development."

Speaking of Burgers and Books, another staff member said, "We no longer just sit and wait for people to come; now we go to them. The staff gets to know the participants who see the library as a friendly place instead of a big building that can be intimidating. We enjoy it because there are so many people participating, and it's neat to see them all leave with books."

Comment

To its funding advantage, the library shows its capability for being a willing player in its contract with local government to serve on community networking teams. It has also put itself in the critical business of children's education to fill gaps not filled by the public schools. Its links with the community and with education should position it favorably for continued local funding. It also agrees to partnerships because they support the library's mission, although they are not library initiated, and it shows its flexibility in revising established procedures to respond to a community need. The response by beneficiaries of the partnership confirms the importance of the community asset. The library is also attuned to alternative sources of funding from which it can benefit and has managed to leverage its asset into the increased use of the library.

It is not clear whether the library is monitoring the budget for its literacy program, for which its partner manages funds. It might agree that no suitable alternative exists to driving "thirty-five miles for burgers." However, because the food portion is said to be a major expense of the program and is funded by grants, the library might be well served to review those costs in the interest of funding. Fiscal conservatism is usually valued by funders, and it could benefit libraries to pare their budget requests.

Notes

1. "Project Manager's Report," CNS, City of Tucson, April 4, 1996.
2. "Project Manager's Report."

Chapter 26

Youth-at-Risk Initiatives: Hamilton Grange Branch of the New York Public Library

> Libraries have failed to connect with such political "hot buttons" as economic development, youth at risk, and public safety.
>
> —Frank Benest, city manager, Brea, California, addressing the Public Library Association Conference, Portland, Oregon, 1996

Branch library income: Not available

In North Harlem, New York City, the Hamilton Grange Branch of the New York Public Library has made a remarkable turnaround. In two years, it went from a raucous hangout dominated by teens who deterred adult users to a respectable and disciplined "oasis," where poetry, plays, and music are valued by many of the same teenagers that had previously caused trouble, according to Josie Harris, a community resident and library user.

Five years later, the number of teenagers who use the library in this economically deprived neighborhood has increased over 100 percent and is now used daily by fifty to sixty teens. Circulation has also increased more than 100 percent, according to branch librarian Sandy Amoyaw, who is credited in large part for the amazing reversal. In 1994, he was awarded the library's second annual Maher-Stern Award for Service Excellence and presented with a $1,000 check to be used for a library service.[1]

Amoyaw's strategy is a lesson in constructive adult-teenager relationships: "I listen to them and so we become friends."[2] According to Marilee Fogelsong, the library's coordinator of young adult services, "Too often we see teenagers as troublemakers; obnoxious and playing loud music. . . . Sandy and his staff treat the teens as adults, young people that they want to have there. Because they treat them with respect, the teenagers give it back." Harris said that it takes "a lot of patience" for the library to serve the neighborhood youths, many of whom are deeply troubled and direct abusive language at the staff. "They tried him many times, but he never let it bother him," said Harris.

Among the innovations of Amoyaw and staff are a three-warning system of rules for using the library that is posted on the tables (e.g., no gum chewing), the recruitment of teen volunteers, and a staff dress code. Collection development has emphasized an expanded young adult collection that has been relocated to occupy center stage at the front of the library (Amoyaw asks teens which books they want) and an African-American section, where people can find their own special books. In addition, an ongoing used book sale on the sidewalk generates enough money to start a circulating video- and audiotape collection. Career and college counseling materials and public Internet access are also part of the branch's resources.[3] Summer reading clubs have been funded by the neighborhood McDonald's and council member Stanley Michels's office. "We try to involve the local politicians as much as possible," said Fogelsong. We'd like to do more with council members, but we're so bogged down with the day to day . . ."

Amoyaw said that the library held a talent show that was produced by the teens, with twenty-five or more "singing and reciting" and giving participants their first experience working together as a team. "We try to be flexible, to get to their level," said Amoyaw, who is "happy when they come to thank us or see us on the street and say 'thank you for giving us this opportunity.'" A senior citizen once handed him $5 to buy a children's book. "This is a very poor neighborhood, and $5 is like a million to the lady who gave it to me."[4]

"Children and teenagers learn to write poetry, play chess, or become a reading club star," said library president Paul LeClerc. "Now this branch has a reputation as a powerful force for community renewal."[5]

According to one user of the branch, twelve-year-old Victor, "This library has helped me a lot in my school years because when I needed information about my projects, I used the encyclopedia to find it. Sometimes when there wasn't enough information in the books, the librarians looked in the Internet to find what I need, with a warm smile on their face."

Comment

"With a warm smile on their face"—how is that for "outstanding public service?" The branch manages to leverage an undesirable community hangout into a community asset: a library that attracts users and, in the process, serves as a positive redirection for neighborhood youth. For this it receives favorable publicity in the form of a library award that attracts the attention of the local press and city council and results in unexpected donations. The library also shows that it can have an impact on the community in other ways, such as providing a role model for teenagers, employing novel and creative ways to implement services, and leveraging book sale funds into new materials that users want. The asset does more than refocus youth; it also contributes to community renewal. It positions the library well to receive future funding and could probably get foundation grants, as community renewal and youth at risk are "hot buttons" of consequence to community funders.

However, it should be noted that donations from businesses that might provide products of questionable benefit to children or children's health—such as some of the McDonald's food products—raise concern among some librarians who discourage library funding from these sources.

Notes

1. "Librarian at Hamilton Grange Recognized for Dynamic Service to Neighborhood Youth," *Staff News* (New York Public Library), vol. 83, no. 51, December 22, 1994, p. 1.

2. Bill Bell, "He Begins New Chapter at Library," *Daily News,* December 12, 1994 (photocopy from the New York Public Library, Community Affairs).

3. "Librarian at Hamilton Grange Recognized . . . ," p. 1.

4. "He Begins New Chapter at Library" (photocopy from the New York Public Library, Community Affairs).

5. "Librarian at Hamilton Grange Recognized . . . ," p. 1.

Chapter 27

Service to the Homebound: Cumberland County Library System, Carlisle, Pennsylvania

> The STAR program is very people oriented, just the opposite of the technology-centered world we live in. The people who deliver the books are like extended families, almost become family. I commend our public library system.
>
> — Nancy Besch, chair, Cumberland County Commissioners

Library income: $2.5 million
Local government share: 43 percent

In a pithy publicity piece distributed at a recent breakfast for county and state legislators, the Cumberland County Library System in Carlisle, Pennsylvania, talked dollars. It claimed that from a $2.2 million budget, it produced a return of $34 million in user services through its eight member libraries, which multiplied community dollars "more than fifteen times." (The library receives 43 percent of its funding from the county and 21 percent from the state.)

Among these services is the STAR (Service to Adult Readers) program, which provides "cost-effective, quality library services for special needs groups, such as homebound and senior facilities' residents."[1] According to STAR volunteer John Sieck, who spoke on the program's behalf at the legislative breakfast, the program's purpose is to serve many of those who would not otherwise have books. Considering that nearly 13,000 items were delivered through the program in one year, the handout noted a contribution of over $300,000 in services. (The figure was based on an average per item cost of $25 for a large-print book and a book on tape.) This did not include the labor provided by STAR volunteers in one-to-one monthly interactions with home-bound clients.

The STAR program is a significant part of the portfolio of services that the system offers. Jonelle Prether Darr, library system director, said that each year at the legislative breakfast, a STAR volunteer speaks about the program, relating personal stories of its clients that are all the more effective coming from volunteers. Following one breakfast, a state legislator unexpectedly gave the library system a donation of $80,000 from discretionary funds. Darr said that she was convinced that although the STAR program was not designated in the gift, it still had a lot to do with the donation. The system's recent selection of a $5,000 software module with specific capability to accommodate STAR is also an indicator of the significance of STAR to the library's portfolio of services that require funding.

Launched with an LSCA (Library Services Construction Act) grant, STAR has since been funded by the system's operating budget. With a collection of over 3,500 large-print books and 1,300 books on tape, annual materials funding is $3,000 for large-print books and $3,500 for audiovisual materials for the years 1995 through 1997.

The STAR program tells as much about the volunteers—63 of them serving 131 clients—as it does about the library system. "Talented people who care are largely responsible for the success of this program," said Darr. According to Nan Cavenaugh, librarian and adult services and STAR coordinator, the national average for the commitment of a volunteer to an organization is six months, whereas some volunteers in the STAR program have been active for ten years—as long as the program has been in existence. They gather information on reader preferences and select and deliver materials to forty-two nursing homes and senior centers, spending at least thirty minutes in social interaction with clients each month. Cavenaugh attributed this participation to the satisfaction that volunteers received from "contributing in a meaningful way to the quality of an individual's life." She said that volunteers ordinarily left the program only if they moved out of the area or were "emotionally drained" following a death or a health change in their client.

Books are selected by the staff, but volunteers select among those that relate to clients' reading preferences and interests as determined by surveys. (The most popular subjects are mysteries, biography, historical fiction, and romance, and the least popular are sports, poetry, music, and science fiction.)[2] Said one client, "It's a wonderful program because you get to read the kind of books you want, so I don't have to take potluck."

Soliciting STAR users or volunteers for library donations was not on the library's current agenda, according to Cavenaugh, who said that administrators did not want the program to be associated by its clients with requests for funds or services to the library. However, Linda Rice, director of the Bosler Free Public Library (budget $400,000), which has the largest STAR program participation of any of the system libraries ("We're in the same building as the system, and they give us pep talks"), said that her library, which raises funds independently of the system, might at some point tactfully approach STAR participants for bequests. "They're in the age-group that is setting up their estates and might see the library as a potential recipient," she said.

The program is not publicized, according to the library. Because participation generally comes by word of mouth, the number served is far below what a county population of 35,000 seniors might generate.[3] According to a supervisor at the county's Area Agency on Aging (a publicly funded organization), the STAR program is "excellent but not being taken enough advantage of. It should be publicized much more." At a library in Allegheny County, Pennsylvania, with a smaller but similar program and where the number of senior citizens (23 percent of residents) is the highest of any county in the United States other than counties in Florida, a staff person said that a reluctance to advertise exists because staffing was inadequate to handle additional users.

One piece of publicity for STAR was a local newspaper story about a ninety-one-year-old client who had a track record of reading twelve books a month for seven years.[4] It was not clear whether the publicity resulted in more users or whether the library could provide enough different books in the reader's favorite subjects, but it was assumed that books were being re-read. Cavenaugh said that all the program's new books were channeled first through this user.

Comment

The library system shows its savvy in legislative advocacy with its distribution of a cost-benefit analysis at a legislative breakfast and recognizes the importance of the STAR program's services to homebound adults as an asset to be leveraged in advocacy. It is also unusually successful in managing a dedicated corps of volunteers on behalf of STAR.

It would seem that the program might be more useful in increasing sorely needed local funding, which, along with other library systems in the state, is among the lowest per capita in the nation. For example, an urban library in the Midwest considers its relationship with a retirement residence a "mutually contributory" partnership. The residence provides space for a branch library's adult programming for the public and in exchange receives programming for its residents. On an individual service basis, it would seem that those who are capable of using library services are also capable of making a contribution to these services in whatever way they can, and they might even recognize it as a form of discrimination for not being asked.

The creativity of librarians in arriving at feasible resolutions for many situations is constantly being challenged and, more often than not, delivers with flying colors.

Notes

1. Cumberland County Library System, "Goal I, Objective 5," *Focus on the Future: Summary,* June 19, 1995, p. 7.

2. Cumberland County Library System, "Homebound Clients Served—Survey," November 1990 (copy of one handwritten sheet, provided by Cavenaugh).

3. Data for ages 60 and over from the 1990 U.S. census for Cumberland County, Pennsylvania.

4. Dan Miller, "Nonagenarian Enlivens Today with Tales of Yesteryear," *The Sentinel* (Carlisle, Pa.), June 10, 1995, p. D2.

Chapter 28

Conclusion

> The best economic development tool is a government that puts a priority on long-term investment in education and public goods and that efficiently delivers the amenities—safe streets, libraries, parks—that citizens value. Creating that kind of government . . . is the way local economies develop and citizens prosper.
>
> —"A View from Elsewhere," editorial, *Sacramento Bee,*
> quoted in *Telegram-Tribune* (San Luis Obispo County, Calif.)
> (photocopy from the San Luis Obispo City-County Library)

A number of ways in which library assets work for funding advantage are illustrated in the preceding accounts and summarized in this chapter. Because assets normally carry possibilities for leveraging to benefit their owners, library assets can be leveraged into stronger assets for funding advantage. However, several factors can prevent the ability of libraries to leverage their assets for financial or other benefit. These include a lack of awareness of the asset's benefit to library stakeholders, an unwillingness to risk funds in hand without the assurance that more funds will result, a lack of time or interest to be concerned with this form of advocacy, a lack of imagination, or a lack of awareness of leveraging possibilities. However, the responsibility of managing an asset includes the requirement of nourishing its growth and usefulness, and this can affect the management of library assets in the future.

From the information provided in the preceding accounts of current library practice, the guidelines for library assets in promoting funding advantage are identified as follows:

Library Management

- The asset is managed according to a special policy authorized by the library or by other professionals knowledgeable in the subject area.

- Specially trained staff are assigned to developing the asset.
- The asset demonstrates the continued support of the library administration and board.
- The asset supports and enhances the library's mission.

Library Response to Community

- The asset responds to a community need.
- The asset responds to more than one community need.
- The asset has incorporated substantial community support in its implementation.
- The structure of the asset is flexible to meet the community's changing needs.

Library Service

- The asset provides services over and beyond conventional library services.
- The asset provides better service relative to other services of its kind.
- Users of the asset indicate their approval.
- The asset increases library usage.
- The asset is indispensable to its users.
- The asset employs creative ways of implementation.

Library Publicity

- The asset is publicized regularly to potential users.
- The asset is well positioned in the library to receive optimal visibility.
- The asset is publicized outside the library community for further benefits.
- The asset has the interest of local politicians.
- The asset is deployed in legislative advocacy.

RULE 5

MIND THE OPPOSITION

Chapter 29

Introduction

> Once lobbying gets into your blood, it's not quite so hard. You become more familiar with people, realize they aren't the ghouls you thought they were.
>
> —Public library director, Allegheny County, Pennsylvania

Most library advocacy efforts focus on educating or informing the public or elected officials about the library to gain their support for library initiatives and, in particular, to win their vote for a library budget or referendum issue. However, efforts of this sort are rarely, if ever, adopted without a certain amount of opposition. If the intent is to get the public's vote, then any lack of willingness to vote yes can be considered opposition and needs to be taken into account.

Ironically, public opposition is not necessarily a negative factor in advocacy. The opposition can unwittingly make positive contributions to an initiative. When the opposition is active, the following can result:

- Library advocates learn more about the library's activities and policies so that they can defend their case.
- Library management learns the public's sentiments regarding library policy.
- Public support is expanded and strengthened.
- Library supporters adopt some of the oppositions' legitimate tactics for their own advocacy (e.g., perseverance and looking at the issues on multiple dimensions).
- Library advocates identify specific members of the opposing ranks (e.g., board members or planning advisers) whom they target for library service.

The positives are not to underestimate the negatives of library opposition. Even without the defeat of an initiative, which is the most obvious downside of the opposition, more library time and effort are often required than originally expected to come to terms with those in disagreement. The library might also be responsible for raising funds for fees—those of attorneys, public relations, and other consultants—to prepare its case. In the worst outcome, a far stronger opposition emerges as a result of the public fracas. These positives and negatives hanging on the presence of library opposition prompt libraries to plan their tactics carefully if they want to keep their initiatives on target.

Hard as it might be, examining the role of the opposition in the light of its potential for facilitating rather than obstructing library initiatives can be productive. Doing so permits library advocates to deal from a position of strength and confidence in their own ability to ride the tide of temporary dissent. As it is a given that "the public loves libraries" ("I'm a great user of the library. I take it for granted, can't imagine it not being there, have kids in school," said a state congressman's assistant), the library is virtually guaranteed a strong support base. However, various politically and economically driven issues can come into play that consume library supporters so that they lose sight of the fact that the public loves libraries, thinking that it has been forever washed over the spillway. Consequently, they react out of fear (thus defeating their efforts) rather than from a willingness to wait out the rough times constructively.

An important quality of public library advocacy might be called "constructive endurance." This devotes time to the airing of negative concerns and treats them in the light of objectivity without the intervention of personal and subjective considerations. For example, if two groups contest the location of a library, each wanting it located for its own convenience, the spokespersons for constructive endurance ("con ed") would collect all the plus and minus facts of each location and invite the antagonists to discuss the issues on the basis of these criteria rather than on their own personal agendas. Con ed can take longer than arguing and ranting and might cost more money in time and consultants' fees, but it has the advantages of arriving at a solution and avoiding negative media coverage for the library, both of which are priority concerns.

The purpose of the discussion in the following chapters is to illustrate some of the thinking of voters and public funders who oppose library funding initiatives—actively with outspoken disagreement or passively by ignoring them. Because "no" votes do not come with qualifiers (an active "no" works the same on a ballot as a passive "no"), both active and passive "no's" are taken into consideration by public libraries.

Chapter 30

Voter Opposition: Three Towns, Two Oppositions

In three towns of similar size and location, recent voter referenda illustrate not only that voter opposition to library funding is thriving and therefore deserves our consideration but also that the difference between wins and losses can be due not to any fault of demographics but to the library that opts for "constructive endurance."

In town A, a campaign for a bond issue to finance a new public library building was expected to be successful — considered a "fait accompli," according to the librarian. An outside consultant had been hired with previous successes in library and school campaigns in the same geographic area. However, at the last minute — "out of left field," said the librarian — an organized opposition advertised inaccurately that the measure would cost taxpayers more than they had thought and that there were "hidden things the library hadn't told the public." In short, the library had not convinced the community of its credibility, and the bond measure was defeated.

In town B, also with a capital bond issue, a dental practice belonging to a dentist who resided in another city was situated across the street from the library. The dentist did not want library customers using public parking spaces that his clients needed, so he campaigned, again at zero hour just before the vote took place, using the argument of "double taxation" that could hurt the town's elderly who were on fixed incomes. Again the library had not prepared its case well enough, and the bond measure was overwhelmingly defeated.

In town C, library representatives had been shouted down by angry residents at a public meeting two years previously, killing a proposal to improve library services. The library decided to try a different approach this time. Employing the same outside consultant as town A, they held group interviews with some 100 community members eight months in advance of a library referendum. Both positive and negative opinions were aired. Then they listened to mainly opposing arguments at seven public meetings of the library board. When the referendum for a capital bond issue came up for the vote, it passed by a 65 percent majority.

Which of the three libraries learned to manage its opposition for a winning vote?

Library supporters identify two kinds of opposition to library funding initiatives: those who are persuadable and those who are venerable by reason of their dogmatism. The persuadable are, for the most part, issue oriented. Their opposition is based on a concern for the library and the weighing of objective criteria, such as arguing against service to all county residents on the basis of the cost deficits that a library in a similar situation sustained or arguing against the architectural plans for a new library because they call for an unpopular addition in the form of a clock tower. In these cases, it is up to library advocates to convince opponents on reason, not emotion.

On the other hand, the venerable opposition is not persuadable under the usual circumstances. Its agenda is unrelated to that of the library and might be hidden. Because this calls for special strategies on the part of library supporters, it is important to recognize the venerable opposition—and to be on the lookout for it early on—because ignoring it can make its efforts balloon out of control, and catering to it can absorb energies more profitably spent on the issue-oriented opposition. Therefore, a fine line needs to be treaded.

The following are some ways of recognizing venerable opponents to library referenda campaigns:

- They are usually nonusers of libraries and not related to library users, especially to those such as children and adults learning to read, who collectively are likely to have strong public support.
- They are usually nonaffiliates of libraries in other ways, although occasionally a library trustee or Friend is in this category, depending on his or her unique perspective on the issue involved. (One library director claimed that "a lunatic Friend" inserted himself into the library campaign, making the director's job more difficult; in another case, library trustees who were concerned for the possible loss of their own autonomy purposely disrupted meetings.)
- They are often against tax increases of any kind and might be politically active in an organization for this purpose. (e.g., TRIM, a powerful tax-limiting referenda organization in Prince George's County, Maryland, that works against library funding. In a rural Pennsylvania county, a spokesperson for a defeated library referendum attributed the loss to the area's strong antitax climate. "People have always moved here because taxes have been low. They don't want government messing in our pot," she said.)
- They are unable to make a connection between the library's mission of

universal access to ideas and their own lives (i.e., they do not see their lives benefiting from "the common good").

- They are convinced that the library works against their better interests (as the dentist was in the previous example).
- They have personal reasons for opposition that are not related to the library's (e.g., they dislike all authority).
- They are usually not team players.
- They have not voted in recent local elections.
- They undermine constructive efforts on the part of the library to reach solutions (e.g., they find reasons to disrupt community meetings).
- They keep their real agendas secret and focus publicly on other issues.

These criteria are not foolproof, as they can be characteristic of library supporters and the persuadable opposition as well. However, taken in their entirety, they can indicate that the opposition that one is dealing with could be venerable and therefore that special handling techniques are needed. One such technique is patient listening without counterarguments, that is, keeping one's mouth closed and ears open and realizing that no amount of effort will change an opinion and that such opposition should be unobtrusively ignored. Commenting on this kind of opposition, referendum expert Richard B. Hall says, "Even in very close campaigns, it is not wise to try to change the minds of 'No' voters. It is much better to try to find more 'Yes' voters, or to concentrate on the undecided voter and get these last two categories to the polls to vote in favor of the issue."[1]

On the other hand, the persuadable opposition relays the message that it is in need of clarification on certain issues that library advocates realize they need to address. Some examples follow:

- The persuadable opposition does not understand the issues at stake. (They like things the way they are, so why should they pay more taxes for improvements?)
- They think that the library is already funded sufficiently for its purposes. (The library already has a fair share of the city's general fund and also gets private donations. Maybe someone is not managing things well, they argue.)
- They do not like the library's style in handling its initiative. (Library administrators are treating the issue as a given. The suggestions of the community have not been solicited to their satisfaction.)
- They do not feel the need to respond to the library in any way, including voting. (Things will take care of themselves. Those who use the library, not themselves, are the ones who can vote for it.)
- They are not prepared to withstand negative media about the library's proposals. (They did not know that a case could be made against the

proposal, and as they read the newspaper's editorial, it makes sense, so they skip the vote.)

- They are not prepared to withstand negative fallout from other referenda on the same ballot as the library's. (They vote against, for example, school expansion on the same ballot and as a result vote no across the board, including no to the library.)
- They live in a community that has a tax-limiting referendum and use this as an excuse to veto the library's referendum. (The idea of no new taxes is appealing, so why should the library get their vote?)
- They are Friends of the library who think that they have a better solution to funding the library than the library has. (They think that if they vote against the referendum, their solution will be the alternative.)
- They "save" their vote for a competing project (e.g., they vote for the new school building instead of a new library).

These are some of the indicators that motivate library supporters to "get their act in gear" and respond constructively to voter opposition.

Note

1. Richard B. Hall, *Winning Library Referenda Campaigns* (New York: Neal-Schuman, 1995), p. 98.

Chapter 31

How Public Library Advocates Handle Voter Opposition

When the Northport-East Northport Public Library on Long Island, New York (budget $3.7 million) campaigned for a winning bond issue, it identified that one-third of the voters would accept the library's plan, another third would accept the plan if it were more carefully developed and explained ("the persuadable opposition"), and the final third would reject it outright ("the venerable opposition"). "We tried to treat the opposition in such a way that they could not get support—which is to say, we heard them out," said Michael Glennon, trustee board chair. "Two professionals on the consulting team and the library director listened to the opposition, spent time, wore them down, and there was never a public fight," said Glennon.[1]

To improve the level of community understanding, the Northport-East Northport library has an award-winning newsletter that is mailed "to every resident, every month, and takes a lot of energy to develop," said Stephanie Heineman, library director. A four-member editorial board decides the issues to include, for example, essentials of programming, library activities, assessing the library in the community, or simply what needs a reminder, said Heineman. "We give the same information in different forms. We say what's been said 100 times before to people familiar with it as well as those unfamiliar." In other words, they take into account how people process information, which can vary.

The Northport library uses other forms of communication with the local public, such as a bright-ideas box located near the reference desk ("we respond to all") and keeping the two local newspapers informed to maintain a measure of library control over its publicity. In particular, Heineman considers it "essential to be a community activist. You can't expect to sit in the office. You must know your patrons and make sure your staff knows them and lets them know why we're here." During construction and remodeling of two new library buildings, the library worked closely with the nearby residents. "If we can't completely meet their demands, at least they're satisfied we've done the best we can," said Heineman. And the opposition that surfaced at referendum time? Heineman said that the library no longer hears from them. "Most of them realize we went the best route, or at least the best under the circumstances," she said.

In the plans for its new building awaiting voter approval, the Brooks Free Library in Harwich, Massachusetts (budget $196,000), redesigned the floor plan to bring children's and family services to the main floor and move reference and research collections to the second floor. The change helped convince the public to vote in favor of the new building, according to Judy Wallace, library director, who also said that the library reviewed its plans with other department heads in the town (e.g., the planning board and the fire and police departments) and in fact made an agreement with the fire department that it could go first with its ballot referendum. As a result, when the library's time came, the fire department and its constituency lent their support to the campaign.

As to getting out the yes vote, the Lemont Public Library District in Lemont, Illinois (budget $600,000), attributed the no votes on two library referenda to the fact that "Lemont's newer, affluent residents were too busy to vote." Three years later, the library's campaign concentrated on "getting the yes vote out" and generally avoiding the opposition, which this time did not materialize, according to James McGloin, library director. This, and the influx of new residents with "dollars and lots of kids," was effective in getting the referendum passed, said McGloin.

After a referendum failure four years previously at the Toledo-Lucas County Public Library in Toledo, Ohio, the library board reduced the amount at issue by nearly $20 million, organized community focus groups and surveys, and convinced the local newspaper, *The Toledo Blade,* to endorse the proposal. According to David M. Noel, the library's coordinator of marketing and development, the *Blade*'s negative stance on the earlier referendum seemed to "give permission to the public to be against" the issue. The second time around, the library spent more time stating its case. Subsequently, the newspaper published two well-timed supportive editorials, including versions of those editorials in each neighborhood news section relevant to specific library branch improvements.

The library also cultivated the Chamber of Commerce, which did not take a position in the first election but issued a formal endorsement for the second. Yard signs that library patrons could take home and others placed at the "100 busiest traffic intersections," said Noel, were also used to alert voters.

The fact that a library measure that passed overwhelmingly in Pasadena, California, was opposed by both the local newspaper and the Chamber of Commerce illustrates that each situation can vary, and this fact needs to be taken into account in library strategies. What apparently impressed voters in Pasadena was a list of over 1,000 supporters (individuals and representatives of community organizations) that was published in the newspaper and in campaign publicity. An especially vote-winning stroke was the staff's dedication to the campaign of the Pasadena Public Library (budget $7.8 million) in that some 92 percent of staff donated their salary adjustments to raise library revenue. Staff members also gave "an average of ten hours per week of their own time to the campaign."[2] Commenting on a recent referendum that renewed the tax initiative, Susan K. Gegenhuber, community services librarian, said, "Pasadena library staff did not give back our raises this time, but that singular and remarkable action in 1992 continued to appear in letters to the paper and press reports about the tax."[3]

However, what the library does is not significant as a campaign tactic unless it is advertised. The Pasadena library was obviously skillful in knowing what information was likely to influence voters and then publicizing it effectively. Just because information exists does not mean that it can work on behalf of a yes vote. As one librarian said, "We can't do enough public relations."

To sum up how advocates handle the opposition, it is recommended that advocates keep the following four points in mind about the opposition:

1. *The opposition makes more noise than supporters do.* It is no news that people are more likely to express their negative feelings than their positive ones. They assume that everything is okay. If everything is not, they let you know. Those who are repeatedly the most outspoken at the meetings to discuss a controversial issue (e.g., a proposed tax increase or a federated effort in which they fear losing their autonomy) are the ones who are opposed to it. The rest are likely to stay home or remain quiet. Therefore, support for a cause cannot be judged by attendance at meetings. At the same time, support cannot be overestimated because of lack of attendance or outspoken opposition. It might be that the opponents are not convinced that they will be listened to and have given up. Therefore, the following point must be considered.

2. *The opposition has to be convinced that they are heard.* Otherwise, they will become still louder and will begin to grow in numbers. As more people witness the way the opposition is treated by the leading supporters—whether paid attention to and given clear explanations, ignored, or, worse, attacked for their disagreement—those on the fence will move to one side or the other. Therefore, advocates need to convince both the opposition and supporters that the position they have taken is justified.

3. *The opposition will diminish in numbers and quiet down as they are convinced that advocates have thought out their case and are doing the very best they can with the situation.* They will fall off by attrition as they see that the support is reasonable, logical, and fair to all concerned, insofar as that is possible. They might not get the solution they wanted, but they are likely to go along with it as long as they have no

reason to feel that they have been unfairly treated and that their concerns have been accommodated.

4. *Disregarding the first three points by those advocating a position means that the problem in question will remain unsolved.* Advocates whose campaigns have been successful say that they never assume victory, no matter how likely it looks. Too many last-minute surprises can occur at the voting booth. Right up to the vote, they press on in their efforts to convince the opposition.

The occurrence of the venerable opposition—those who are determined to be opposed for reasons unrelated to the issues at hand and therefore try to stall constructive efforts—should not be confused with the persuadable opposition. The venerable opposition should be treated with respect (they are, after all, venerable in their persistence), but it is possible to dispense respect in a "New York minute" without having to take one's time from more productive efforts. Of course, advocates should be sure that that they are assessing the situation accurately, for the venerables might be persuadable after all and therefore deserving of advocates' efforts.

Notes

1. Michael L. Glennon, "Developing and Passing a Bond Issue," *Public Libraries,* January/February 1997, p. 24f.

2. Sally Young and Geni Sowell, "Special Library Tax?" *The Bottom Line,* vol. 7, no. 2 (1993), pp. 8–11.

3. Public Library Association, Pub-Lib listserv, March 17, 1997.

Chapter 32

Ten Reasons Elected Officials Oppose Library Funding

> Chairperson Foster: I am glad to hear that we can renew books by phone. That is going to cost you money, though, isn't it? Mr. LeClerc: Well, we are here to ask for more money, Mr. Chairman. Chairperson Foster: Pardon me?
>
> —New York City Council, *Transcript of the Minutes of the Preliminary Budget Hearing,* New York City, March 12, 1997, p. 8

As voters have reasons for opposing library referenda, local public funders (council members, aldermen, selectmen, commissioners and so on) have their reasons for opposing funds for library budgets. These can reflect both personal feelings and understanding or interpretation of the issues. Some of the reasons given for their opposition are as follows:

1. *"The library should do a better job of relating to the community."* "Some libraries do not care about the community. But if they worked to get the support of a broad spectrum of the community, nurture them on a personal basis, and bring them to the library, they would have little to fear about their funding. There is a direct correlation between the effort made by libraries and their ability to attract funds" (county government official).
2. *"The library should do a better job of customer service."* "I live right across the street from the library, and I am rarely contacted as either a citizen or as a councilman. . . . Not everyone is trained in Dewey decimal systems. It is a childhood trauma for me. I would like more personal service to find the books I want" (city council member).
3. *"Public libraries should combine with school libraries."* "Every time I hear comments about library needs . . . there is never a discussion

on using the resources of community colleges or school libraries"
(state legislator).[1]

4. *"There are other priorities for public dollars."* "I sat down with the
(library) people . . . in December, I told them any new plan would
have to knock the socks off my feet, that the city's families-and-edu-
cation levy was going to be my first priority" (city council member).[2]

5. *"Libraries are already sufficiently funded, especially if they get private dollars."* "City council is not going to tell you directly, but you
pick up from private conversations that they think, since the library
has an endowment, it is OK [can do without more public funds]" (public library director).

6. *"A vote for the library budget will probably not help the council member's reelection."* "I can't afford the luxury to have the people in . . .
[one] branch like me, and the people of . . . [another] branch hate me.
And this is not the time to get anybody to hate me, okay? . . . People
often say, don't be parochial, but we never forget how we got here and
how we will stay here, and this is not the year [election year] to forget that" (city council member).[3]

7. *"A cut to the library's budget can help solve the city's financial
plight."* "The city's new mayor . . . announced that he had looked at
the finances of the city—and that they were worse than he had imag-
ined. The library would have to close because [he] would cut all of its
city funding" (editor of library newsletter).[4]

8. *"The library does not help itself."* "When public officials ask, 'Are
you using volunteers, are you seeking private funding?' what they are
really saying is, 'what are you doing to help yourself?' " (administrator of library Friends).[5]

9. *"There is no return on the dollar when it comes to library funding."*
"City managers view libraries as cost center, as discretionary, not basic services, as a drain on the general fund, and in competition in the
marketplace with bookstores and online services" (city manager).[6]

10. *"Council members do not know what the issues are, nor who the library's supporters are."* "We expect a professional librarian to lobby
us. *They become a resource for us* [emphasis added]. We establish a
relationship. They are a source of information that is reliable and
knowledgeable, a conversation back and forth, not passive [When we
don't have this situation, we don't know what to think."] (assistant to
state legislator).

These statements boil down to a dearth of communication and interrelation-
ships among libraries and local government. Those who are doing the funding
want attention in the form of information and interaction with those asking for
funds. Their concerns fall into three categories:

1. Is the library helping to meet community needs through community teamwork, providing essential materials, and good customer service?
2. Is the library stretching tight community dollars through partnerships, cost savings, and private sources of income?
3. Is the library helping elected officials do their jobs better through shared constituencies, publicity opportunities, and providing up-to-date and accurate information?

The library's communication in response to these issues can determine its funding. The following chapter gives an example of constructive response at a library budget hearing.

Notes

1. Public Library Association, Pub-Lib listserv, September 6, 1996.
2. Gordy Holt, "My Turn, Says the Seattle Public Library," *Seattle Post Intelligencer,* March 17, 1997 (photocopy provided by the Seattle Public Library, Community Relations).
3. New York City Council, *Transcript of the Minutes of the Preliminary Budget Hearing,* New York City, March 12, 1997, p. 42.
4. New York Public Library Association, "Training," *NYLA PR Alert,* fall 1997, p. 2.
5. "Libraries for the Future," Pub-Adv listserv, May 7, 1997.
6. Gordon Flagg, "PLA Prospers in Portland," *American Libraries,* May 1996, p. 13.

Chapter 33

Anatomy of a Library Advocacy Case for Public Funding: Budget Hearings

When the three megalibraries of the New York City system—the New York Public Library, Queens Borough Public Library, and the Brooklyn Public Library—made their individual cases at the city's preliminary budget hearings, their presentations addressed the following concerns of city council members (editorial license in interpreting the presentations is in bracketed quotes):

- *People-related numbers—numbers of users, numbers of circulating items, numbers that increased over the previous years, and numbers of others, such as parents and teachers indirectly affected by certain programs.* In eighty minutes of testimony, forty-two people numbers were quoted. ["With so many of your constituents using the library or related to users, your vote for the library budget can help your reelection campaign."]
- *Dollar-related numbers—the estimated costs of each of the new or upgraded programs in the library's proposed budgets.* ["We are credible players, not just picking fancies out of the air. We know how to talk dollars."]
- *The library's provision for new members of the community, such as immigrants.* ["We are team players in this community, responding to needs as we can."]
- *The library's help for schools and children—that is, "de facto school issues" and latchkey programs.* ["We respond to needs of other institutions, especially the schools."]
- *Other sources of income, such as federal and private grants.* ["We do not depend only on your largess—we are supplementing it with our own efforts."]

- *The library's "strategic directions."* ["We are not playing sandlot football, we are serious players."]
- *The effects of the economy.* ["We're doing the best we can, but as victims of inflationary times, we need your help."]
- *"Thank you very much"—thank you for your past support, thank you for your questions, thank you for your clarification, thank you for your response.* In eighty minutes of testimony, there were thirty-three thank you's. ["By expressing our gratitude publicly in this and other forums, we hope to lay the groundwork for continuing this partnership—you give us the funds we ask for, and we repeatedly acknowledge them publicly so that you get the response you need to help you do your job and keep your public image intact, this being an election year, ahem."]

Council members were also interested in other input relevant to the libraries' funding requests, such as how the present level of library service would be affected were additional money not forthcoming ["It would deteriorate"], the costs of bridging deficiencies in the public schools, ["Have not been calculated"], the results of the CLASP (Connecting Libraries and Schools Project) program in terms of improvement in reading and other academic achievements ["All results to date are "anecdotal, no formal results"]. The council members probably did not expect the library to have the costs-and-results studies that they referred to, but by bringing up the subject they indicated their interest in the submission of analytical data in addition to the libraries' anecdotal and word-of-mouth reports. By going on record with these questions, council might be giving notice that analytical data might assume more importance in future funding considerations and that libraries should be forewarned.

Chapter 34

What Elected Officials Want from Public Library Supporters

The office of Pennsylvania State Representative Ivan Itkin provided the following information for the benefit of library advocates who want to communicate more effectively with public funders. From these advocates, Itkin's staff (as well as other public officials) want the following:

- "The usual statistics on users and purchases."
- "Intangibles, such as what services the library is providing and who benefits, what local needs the library is filling, what makes a difference to whom, and where the money goes."
- "Letters with detailed information about what is happening in the library's local community."
- "Face-to-face contact."
- "Invitations to the library, especially if there is a media opportunity."
- "Maybe show us a video about what's going on—that libraries aren't stuffy places anymore."
- "Be prepared with answers to our questions. Don't assume we know more than we do."
- "Conciseness. We have a staff of eight, and we get about 100 letters a week at budget time—not counting the 1,000 on a single topic that people were asked to write. Write your letters from a personal approach—that is, 'I live next door to the library, and this program is great for . . . '."
- "Get to know our staff. They can guide you through the maze, not only funds but regulatory and other interests. It helps us if one person is recognizable as the main person, perhaps the director or an association head."
- "Let us know what gets people into the library. How is the library connected to the community?"

- "Don't ask us just for money. Ask also for time, energy, ideas, planning, and presenting programs, when applicable. Send us invitations to events; for example, the legislator was asked to present an award at a kids' drawing contest. See that we get into the physical plant."
- "We like to know if you can tap into private funding. It demonstrates your capability to leverage public funds. If a matching element is involved, all the better. We like public and private funds complementing each other."
- "Tell us what will happen if the money is not there—that is, kids with this need are not being served, which leaves a hole in the social fabric. For example, at Drexel University, if their cooperative education program is eliminated, then an income of $19 million will be cut, which profited from an investment of $5 million. The program creates jobs—75 percent have jobs before they graduate. It makes the program unique. Show us what is unique about the library you represent."
- "We like the idea of partnering. Tell us when there are other organizations with whom you share goals, team up, and work together."
- "Also, it helps to have local business on your side, so let us know about that."

The legislator provides several ways of helping library supporters make their case before public officials. The next chapter provides a list of current practices by U.S. public library advocates that outlines most of these ways.

Chapter 35

How Public Library Advocates Respond to Public Funders

The following activities of public library supporters address public officials' needs for communication with the library to better understand how it is helping the community, how it stretches community dollars, and how it helps public officials do their jobs better. Public library advocates do the following to communicate effectively with public officials:

- Meet personally with their local funding officials about four times a year.
- Thank public officials regularly and publicly for their past support.
- Send personal postcards or letters—not forms—indicating library support.
- Send Valentines made by local schoolchildren. The Brooklyn Public Library appears to have originated this idea.
- Send library newsletters and videos describing library activities.
- Invite public officials to library events.
- Solicit Friends, board members, local business interests, and teens to testify on behalf of the library.
- Discuss the library's long-range plans.
- Issue press releases about the library's activities for widest possible publication.
- Provide human interest stories about the library.

Advocates do the following to show how the library helps meet community needs:

- Publicize numbers—numbers of users, numbers of items that are circulated, numbers of people who enter the library, and estimated numbers of people who are affected by various library programs.

- Emphasize the library's literacy programs.
- Emphasize the library's services to young children.
- Emphasize the library's services to schoolchildren.
- Emphasize the library's services to non-English-speaking users.
- Emphasize the library's access to the information highway to help the "have-nots."
- Explain how the loss of library open hours would affect library customers.

Advocates do the following to show how the library stretches community dollars:

- Publicize grants and other donations.
- Publicize dollars leveraged for more dollars or for in-kind benefits.
- Publicize community partnerships.
- Include program budgets in budget presentations to clarify fund requests.
- Talk money—quantifying library services to show in dollar values what the library produces from the dollars it receives.
- Show how the library has cut costs.
- Make friends with members of local organizations and representatives of public services that might compete for funds to promote consolidated efforts.

Advocates do the following to show how the library helps public officials do their jobs better:

- Provide recent information about the library and its programs in an easily referenced format to facilitate the officials' use of the information in press releases and other public comments that make him or her "look good."
- Look for ways in which library resources can be of service to public officials, such as alerting them to library information and materials relevant to their work and setting up home pages for them on the Internet.
- Keep informed about public officials' backgrounds and preferences and competing or related funding initiatives to customize library requests.
- Ask public officials to present the awards in schoolchildren's summer reading programs.
- Invite public officials to hold public meetings at the library.
- Initiate studies to respond to future needs of public officials for comparative costs between current activities and possible alternatives.

Not only do public library advocates engage in these activities to thwart potential opposition from public officials, but, as the next chapter describes, they are also diligent in laying a groundwork of library support among community leaders well before any opposition is even aware of itself!

Chapter 36

Responding to the Opposition before It Takes Root: Library Advocacy and Community Boards at the New York Public Library

> Our staff representatives to the community boards are an extremely effective part of our advocacy.
>
> —Suzanne C. Mueller, New York Public Library trustee, at a library board meeting, April 17, 1996, on the eve of the opening of the library's Science, Industry and Business Library (SIBL) (The city council provided $13 million for the new library as a result of the library's advocacy and success in raising private funds.)

Library participation in local community board meetings in New York City and in similar organizations elsewhere is an informal and effective way for library representatives to interact face to face with elected officials. In this context, it can also demonstrate the library's accountability to the community in shaping services for which funds are subsequently requested. In New York City, library participation in these meetings came about as a result of the citywide budget crisis that affected the library in the mid-1970s.

Monthly community board meetings in New York can attract up to fifty board member-volunteers appointed by local city officials plus local council members, state legislators, neighborhood schmoozers, and gregarious others—including public library representatives who might also be board members. The fifty-nine community boards in the city's five boroughs function as advisors to city government, and because they are products of the particular neighborhood in which they are located, they reflect the unique characteristics of their slice of the city.

The event, which resembles a town meeting, is considered by some attendees among the best forms of entertainment in the city. On the agenda at a three- to four-hour meeting of community board #5—whose mid-Manhattan jurisdiction includes the New York Public Library's (NYPL's) landmark building at Fifth Avenue and Forty-second Street and two of its eighty-two branches, Grand Central Terminal, and the south portion of Central Park—were approvals of requests for street fairs, a presentation of a redesign proposal of the Central Park Children's Zoo, a landmark application for Grand Central Terminal, and a proposed location for a school of performing arts. These were sandwiched among compliments to a new mother and board member with her newborn in tow, announcement of the home address to send get-well wishes to an absentee (an NYPL representative), welcome-back greetings to a local priest and board member returned from sabbatical, ongoing visits to the refreshment table, and reunions with friends and elected officials.

Such happenings in this city, where news is nothing if not current, can be a librarian's manna, enabling him or her to access the news before the news and, back home at the NYPL, to contact the regional librarian or department of government relations to set the appropriate wheels turning in response. "We plug into where the city is going at the time," said Bonnie E. Williams, NYPL administrative librarian and community board veteran, who spends up to half her job in various community interactions. "We tell our story and listen for issues of interest or importance to supervisors or regional librarians."

One example of advocacy success is that the library has sought funding for a new borough center in the Bronx for more than two decades. According to Williams,

> Throughout 1995–1996, members of the . . . library's support group with the branch librarian . . . visited all twelve Community Boards in the Bronx to ask for their support in City budget priorities for a new Bronx Library Center. They explained what the Bronx needed was a new building that would improve and increase library service to the entire Borough. . . . Ten of the twelve boards made a new Center a priority for capital funds in FY 97–98. . . . This year, the Mayor . . . the Borough President and the Bronx City Council delegation, all designated funds to begin the process of finding a site and preliminary design.[1]

Bronx public officials provided a combined $8 million for the $14.5 million project.[2]

Required attendance at monthly community board meetings was instituted for all professional NYPL librarians in the 1970s at the time of the city's fiscal crisis. Written into job descriptions, it is performed on the staff member's own time. "How else will the community know what we are doing, and how can we find out what they need if we aren't there?" asked Williams, whose institution has been going into housing projects and reaching out to immigrants for a record 100 years.

According to an in-house advocacy manual, the *Budget Action Handbook* (see its listings in appendix 2), which is distributed to all NYPL librarians, each board has its own chairperson, a district manager, and "distinct structure and practices." Librarians coordinate their attendance with one another for monthly board meetings and interim committee meetings. The handbook urges them to "develop a good working relationship with the district manager," actively participate in the board's activities, get acquainted with other members individually, encourage the board to form a library committee or subcommittee, arrange for people to testify in support of the library at board budget hearings, encourage the board to pass resolutions or write letters to public officials in support of libraries, invite board members to tour the library, thank board members for their support of the library, invite them to library events, and coordinate and report all activities to the regional librarian and government relations representatives.

At the community boards, oral presentations of the library budget are made by the staff library representatives at the time that budget priorities are submitted to the city.

Judging from the track record, library representation pays dividends when librarians sit monthly at the same table with their elected officials. The latter avoid cutting back hours for libraries in their districts and reach into their discretionary funds to help. For example, in fiscal year 1997, council members provided discretionary funds ranging from $50,000 to $3 million for capital improvements at their respective branch libraries. At community board #5, council member Ronnie Eldridge donated $538,000 for renovation of a branch library in her jurisdiction. Library administration do their part to keep the ball moving by providing details of council members' donations to all staff, including community board representatives.[3]

"What you put out comes back to you," said Williams. "Local users, library, council members . . . we've built this up over years. . . . Who says local support doesn't work?"

Notes

1. Letter from Bonnie Williams to the author, March 12, 1997.
2. Memorandum to the branch libraries from the branch library director, NYPL, July 10, 1996.
3. Memorandum to the branch libraries.

Chapter 37

Conclusion

From community board meetings to a variety of written, verbal, and face-to-face means, public library advocates send a continual message to their public that they are willing to listen and, when necessary, respond constructively to the opposition. Providing information to the public is the library's stock in trade, so providing the information in support of its initiatives requires a major overhaul not in library thinking but rather in procedures and priorities. Any institution should be able to justify its reasons for existence to those who need to know and on whom it depends for funding. Public officials attempting to do their jobs of helping meet community needs, stretching community dollars, and performing their duties better (often with an eye to reelection or other community perks) need the contribution of public libraries to these efforts. The more the library can produce the needed results, the better the library's chances of getting the funds it needs.

In the process, advocates heighten their own awareness and definition of library needs and goals, helping to prepare the library for a future in which public relationships are an indispensable ingredient to successful funding.

RULE 6

CREATE AND INNOVATE

Chapter 38

Introduction

> When we asked an international corporation to donate funds to our
> new library, we pointed out that the building would be located on
> the site of the longest homerun in baseball history that Williams hit
> when he was playing for the Padres. The ball landed on a freight
> train and ended up in Los Angeles 100 miles north of here.
>
> —San Diego Public Library administrator

> Necessity is the mother of invention.
>
> —Richard Franck, *Northern Memoirs* (n.p.: 1658), p. 44 (from
> the reference service at the Carnegie Library of Pittsburgh)

Creative and innovative tactics that library advocates devise in the current economic and social climate grow out of the strategies discussed in the previous chapters—thinking change, making teamwork and partnering efforts, managing library assets, and dealing with the opposition. Creativity and innovation take into account the library's resources in its mission, staff, collections, services, programs, environment, and constituencies: board members, public and private funders, Friends, local institutions, businesses, and library users.

For the purposes of this discussion, creativity is using library resources in ways that are unconventional or untraditional to benefit library advocacy and its objective: library funding. In the context of library funding, creativity has several outcomes:

1. It changes traditional forms (e.g., service outlets, contracts, and the involvement of stakeholders).
2. It changes thinking and practice (e.g., calculating cost-benefit studies or extended hours of opening for their political benefit).

3. It calls attention to the library in the local and national media.
4. It results in new or renewed funds.
5. It helps position the library favorably for funding.
6. It spurs other creative efforts.
7. It changes the library culture.
8. It wins awards (e.g., library newsletter awards).

When asked whether his library had creative ways of obtaining funds, a librarian in a midsize library said that it was "pretty humdrum" in that respect, just the usual bake sales and annual appeals. Because the name of the game is funding, "humdrum" might be just the ticket if it works for funding purposes. The difference between approaching funding in a humdrum fashion and approaching it "creatively" is often determined by the presence of a budget crisis.

When a library budget is severely threatened with diminution or extinction, as in regions of tax-limiting legislation or bankrupt public treasuries, the emergency escape routes to funding creativity begin to hatch, encouraged by library administrators and Friends groups. Then libraries start reaching out to their communities with serious intent, circulating questionnaires for community feedback, looking at library resources from the perspective of community needs, developing long-range plans, searching for partnerships that consolidate funds or stimulate future funding, and cultivating relationships with local funding officials.

An impetus to creative and innovative funding can be a matter of having the collective wherewithal—the interest, the time, and the know-how—or a matter of needing to be prepared for possible funding setbacks in the future. Another impetus might be that changing things can make the job more fun, or perhaps someone read this book and knew that they could devise funding solutions at least as good as those presented here.

Finding new funding sources in the hope of avoiding budget crises brings its own problems. When libraries begin looking at alternative funding, a concern arises that public funders will take their part less seriously or even opt out entirely. After all, public funders are the original "partners" and should be treated as such. (The euphemism "partners" can backfire when too casually used.) As no player wants to be on the bench when he or she has been in the starting lineup, it is up to the library partner to pave the way with primary funders and partners when they seek to bring new players into the ball game. (See the discussion of the Chicago Public Library in the next chapter.)

Therefore, creative and innovative tactics on the part of library advocates are a response not only to crisis intervention but also to efforts to offset such crises.

Chapter 39

Ways in Which Public Library Advocates Are Creative and Innovative for Funding Advantage

Some of the ways in which libraries are creative in altering convention and tradition for funding advantage refer to the field accounts described earlier in this book. Here are some examples:

1. *They introduce a project that attracts funders.* Development of the Electronic Information Network (EIN) project at the Carnegie Library of Pittsburgh (chapter 11) was inspired largely by the fact that the library could not get funding for its materials budget. The idea to link some forty county libraries and to create public Internet access and the way in which it was marketed were the masterstrokes that captured public and private funds to support the library's collections. Because the approach was novel, funders rose to the occasion.

2. *They adopt for library purposes what is already up and running.* When community activists sat in to protest library cuts and the closing of a branch library during New York City's funding crisis in the 1970s, New York Public Library (chapter 9) administrators realized that the activists provided a resource that could be tapped. Since then, thousands of volunteers have been recruited to intercede with public officials on behalf of the library. Having suffered defeat of a previous library referendum, the Friends of the Oakland Public Library (chapter 15) engaged the local chapter of the employees union the second time around because the union had the necessary skills, publicity, and phone bank facilities already in operation to launch a successful campaign on the library's behalf.

3. *They leverage gift dollars to get more dollars.* When the Central Arkansas Library System (chapter 20) in Little Rock, Arkansas, received a grant from Microsoft Corporation for the Libraries Online! project, it set up a bookmobile service to community centers and housing projects in underserved areas that

combined books and public Internet access computers. With Microsoft dollars in hand, it was able to attract funds from the Department of Housing and Urban Development (HUD), the Rockefeller Trust, and a local foundation for a total project funding of $138,000.

4. *They implement politically correct initiatives.* Programs (such as Little Rock's) to benefit the underserved, the Friends of the St. Paul Public Library's partnerships (chapter 18) with nonprofits that serve minority-owned businesses, and the Tucson-Pima Library's (chapter 25) literacy and homework center programs attract funding because they support public and private funding agendas for socially responsible initiatives.

5. *They turn entertainment into library funding.* The Friends of the Reading Public Library's (chapter 17) seventeen-plus years of annual used-book sales have earned over a million dollars from which library programs have benefited. The fact that reading is associated with libraries might give this project a natural marketing edge, as does the city's and library's name: Reading.

6. *They mix unconventional materials with the conventional.* The Kokomo-Howard County Public Library's (chapter 24) museum-quality fine art collection serves as a unique community resource not likely to be found in other public libraries. Moreover, it is a project that has continued to grow and develop for half a century, serving and stimulating the community's aesthetic needs and drawing attention to the library beyond the immediate locale.

7. *They develop unconventional library services.* The Toledo-Lucas County Public Library's (chapter 23) Government Procurement Center not only brings in dollars to the community, as it was originally set up to do, but also has built on the original plan to incorporate consulting and research services, giving the library good marks in a business-oriented community.

8. *They turn an unconventional library audience into a conventional one.* The Hamilton Grange branch of the New York Public Library (chapter 26) has managed to convert trouble-causing teenagers into promising, well-behaved, run-of-the-mill library users.

In addition to examples from the field accounts, other creative efforts of libraries to facilitate advocacy and funding are the following:

1. *They develop new structures.* The San Francisco Public Library's (chapter 2) affinity groups and the Carnegie Library of Pittsburgh's ad hoc teams are examples of new structures for advocacy. The affinity groups are a way of attracting donations from various ethnic and other interest groups as contributions to special library collections. In San Francisco, they addressed, on the one hand, the preference of library donors to give for some specific cause and, on the other, library needs for undesignated dollars. They did this by tying in with the donation to the special collection a required portion for the new main's (central building) general fund. The affinity group idea is thought to have saved the new main's campaign, as it contributed to nearly one-third of the campaign funds either directly or through matching grants. One caveat, however, is that

affinity groups can complicate fund-raising because they require campaign managers to deal with multiple fund-raising entities as each group manages its own campaign.

The ad hoc advocacy teams that originated in Pittsburgh to focus on city and county funders are designed to involve a variety of advocacy voices—trustees, Friends, and library staff—supposedly one of each per team. They meet with public officials three times per year and consider the effort useful in, for example, informing city council of obligations to fund library capital costs (often ignored in the past) and in getting public officials to visit the library. They are careful to keep records of the costs spent in advocacy activities to document that they are not overstepping the line between "simple" advocacy and "lobbying," on which legal restraints exist for a nonprofit tax-exempt organization. They also need to devise ways to overcome declining interest on the part of team members from one year to the next. On the other hand, the mix of library supporters—trustees, staff, and Friends—makes for a more dynamic impact than any one entity alone could do, and such a blend can ignite ideas for future collaborative efforts.

2. *They mobilize the grassroots.* Community residents of the Rockridge area of Oakland, California, mobilized when the Rockridge branch of the Oakland Public Library had a severe rent increase that threatened the library's existence. Grassroots efforts, facilitated by a popular neighborhood newsletter, were able to establish a voter-approved special tax district. Using local support as a leverage, additional funding was received from a state library grant, city-donated land, and community philanthropy for a total $3.8 million. The state support was especially difficult to obtain. The fact that it succeeded is believed, ironically, to be due to a neighborhood tragedy: a devastating fire that swept through the area, causing loss of lives and homes just prior to the state's library grant voting session. Advocates who were present at the voting wore identification tags with a red flame, emphasizing the function of a new library as a community center—something for which the fire tragedy had demonstrated a serious need.

3. *They locate service outlets in high-traffic areas.* Requiring space for a library branch to serve a rural area, but without the funding to make it possible, Adams Memorial Library (income $376,000) in Latrobe, Pennsylvania, arranged with a local supermarket in a busy mall to provide 6,000 square feet of donated space within the market. For the public who loves libraries, this novel stroke was news. It attracted national media coverage in the *Wall Street Journal* (June 3, 1996), *USA Today* (June 5, 1996), and several other publications. A similar, older but smaller facility is in Wichita, Kansas, where a branch of the Wichita Public Library (income $5.2 million) has been located in a nationally affiliated supermarket for ten years. It recently renewed its contract. Both facilities compare favorably with other branches of their libraries in terms of use. Because the branches have shorter hours than their supermarket hosts, this poses minor problems. The Wichita branch finds that some of its returned

videos disappear from their designated drop-off point. On the other hand, the Latrobe branch is concerned with an occasionally incompatible mix of the branch patrons with those of an adjoining child day-care center. The supermarket ownership has also changed hands, but so far this has not interfered with the Latrobe library's facility.

4. *They develop entrepreneurial ventures.* Friends of the Minneapolis Public Library (income $16.8 million) were one of the first to establish a used bookstore to handle the withdrawn books from its fourteen branches as well as some book donations. In operation for fourteen years as part of the library's main facility, it yields over $100,000 per year to benefit such things as the library's Franklin Learning Center (an adult literacy center) and is thought to save the library extensive costs in used-book disposal, according to its executive director.

5. *They take an activist stance.* Along with other colleagues heading up small municipal libraries in the county, the director of the McKeesport Public Library (income $389,000) in McKeesport, Pennsylvania, learned that a proposal for a tax to benefit county assets such as museums and sports facilities did not include as beneficiaries the forty or so municipal libraries in the county that were suffering tremendous budget crises following the demise of the local steel industry. Consequently, a small group of librarians in the county concentrated their efforts for a year to lobby the municipalities and county government to ensure that all the county libraries would be included in the new tax funding. Their case was won largely because the legislation for the tax needed state approval. To pass, the pending tax required the votes of representatives of small municipalities that had no sports arenas or museums in their districts to benefit from it but that did, luckily, have public libraries that could benefit. Rewriting the legislation to include municipal libraries ensured enough yes votes to pass the measure and to benefit the libraries in a backdoor kind of move.

6. *They make written contracts and other legal agreements with local government.* The Palm Springs Public Library (income $1.6 million) in Palm Springs, California, contracted with the City of Palm Springs to provide certain designated library services, including hours of service (fifty-five hours per week), acquisitions ($215,000), collection development, staffing, and automation if the city would in turn provide funding for five years in the annual amounts that the library specified (see item 7 in appendix 2). According to the city librarian, this enables the city council to plan its future, the library's customers to be comfortable with the fees they pay, and the library to have "more authority over its destiny." Other benefits, as outlined in a memo to the city council, are long-term quality library services, recycling of unexpended funds in the interests of cost conservation, coordination of fee increases with service enhancements, a simpler annual budget process, and improved planning opportunities for both the city council and the library.

Another agreement, in the form of a city ordinance, was arranged by the Chicago Public Library to offset concerns that the library foundation's private fund-raising might jeopardize public funding. The ordinance calls for the city council to consider private funding "as an additional, not an alternative, source of revenue" and to ensure that an increase in private funding "will not be the basis or justification for offsetting reductions in public funding" (see item 8 in appendix 2).

7. *They broaden funding responsibility.* The usual practice in public library funding is for public funding to cover capital costs and operations, including human resources, and private funding to cover enhancements, such as computer workstations and special collections. However, when the funding situation is so critical that public funding cannot support capital costs and operations (as it has been in California and other places burdened with tax-limiting legislation), advocates look to other means of support for the basics. For example, the San Luis Obispo City-County Library (income $3.8 million) in San Luis Obispo, California, invited Friends groups and service organizations to shoulder the expenses of extended open hours in the branch libraries. Sometimes private donations are matched or supplemented by donations from public officials or community councils. The library has also approached public entities, such as school districts, in the hope of achieving more stable sources of funding than private donations can deliver.

At the New York Public Library, the Adopt a Branch program matches private donors with local philanthropic individuals willing to donate $500,000 to be matched by grants from local elected officials of $1 million or more to restore branch libraries, especially in Harlem and the Bronx, which have been badly in need of repair.[1]

Some library advocates do not approve of the practice of private contributions funding what has traditionally been the responsibility of public funders. Public funding, they say, might not be easily reestablished, as too many other public service demands are made on public general funds, which do not have the alternative of private funding. If the library is resourceful in raising private funds, public funders will insist that it continue this way, so the argument goes.

8. *They discover off-the-wall funding sources.* The Commission on the Future of Libraries in Allegheny County, Pennsylvania, receives funds for its Knowledge Connections project—consisting of minilibraries with computer capabilities located in public housing communities—from a special fund generated by forfeiture fees from illegal gambling operations, such as raids on sports betting and numbers operations, lotteries, and video poker machines. In two years, the fund has yielded $105,000.[2]

The Auberry branch of the Fresno County Free Library (income $5.8 million) in Fresno, California, convinced its Chamber of Commerce to ask a bank that was closing its local branch to donate the bank building for a new Internet-capable library and community meeting center. The bank agreed to donate the 5,024-square-foot building and also threw into the package the furniture and computer systems and over an acre of land on which the building stands for a total donation valued at over $500,000. In the opinion of a Friends member, the gift was made possible "because the Chamber had the guts to ask for it," suggesting that the same can be true for other libraries if they take the initiative.[3]

The Mechanicsburg Area Public Library (income $293,000) in Mechanicsburg, Pennsylvania, gets income from used ink-jet and laser cartridges that they deposit with a local print cartridge company that recycles the cartridges. The going rate is $3 for a laser cartridge and $1 for an ink-jet cartridge. In the first few months, the library received $200 (enough to pay the monthly telecommunications bill of some libraries). They expect receipts to increase as word gets around about this way of donating to the library.

9. *They convince other public agencies to help.* The Patterson Public Library (income $191,000) in Westfield, New York, has an answer to libraries concerned about the unrecovered costs that a public library sustains in serving schoolchildren. The library has a partnership with the local school system in which it reports its services annually: 209 children's program sessions, 27 teen program sessions, 1,597 summer youth program sessions, plus a number of new acquisitions for children and site visits to schools. The school responds by donating an agreed-on annual fee—currently $11,000, up from $9,000 a few years ago in this town of 5,000 people. The library also includes school staff on the library board to help cement the partnership.

10. *They calculate cost benefits.* With a $2.2 million income, the Cumberland County Library System (chapter 27) in Carlisle, Pennsylvania, calculated a return of $34 million in user services and therefore multiplied community dollars "more than fifteen times." This information was presented to local funders. Reasoning that public libraries could use some cost-recovery assistance from the IRS and other taxing agencies for distributing gratis federal and other tax forms and thereby saving these agencies huge amounts of money at the expense of public libraries, the Oak Lawn Public Library (income $2.9 million) in Oak Lawn, Illinois, did what any library advocate might constructively do on behalf of what is being advocated: They calculated the costs of the service involved in terms of labor (that of the director, department heads, supervisors, pages, and public relations) and space and utilities and came up with a grand total of $6,245.85 for a hypothetical public library to distribute all tax forms (local, state, and federal). Step-by-step instructions for this "tax form distribution assessment" are posted on the Internet for libraries to figure their own costs. It is not yet clear what the next steps are to actual cost recovery, but cost-benefit analyses can be potent weapons that are expected to be of greater necessity in future advocacy.[4]

11. *They broadcast their views.* Public library advocacy is the subject of a number of listservs available to library administrators, Friends, and the public through e-mail subscription (see the bibliography). One recent interchange between library administrators illustrates the kind of debate that the advent of li-

brary advocacy has stimulated. This debate pertains to the value that libraries place on outstanding public service in terms of funding cuts:

> Viewpoint 1. When asked in budget deliberations what I would do if asked to cut $10,000 from my budget, my answer (as an administrator) was always "cut Sunday hours." Why? Well . . . if you are being asked to take a cut, make it something which will be visible . . . not one less staff member here and there, and a few fewer books.
>
> Viewpoint 2. Do you "hit 'em where it hurts" and cut the busiest weekend hours when working parents and their kids can come to the library so that the impact draws political flak upon the budget cutters, or do you try as best you can to cut hours which are less active and/or services which have seen declining or limited use? . . . The upset tax payers who find the library doors closed and locked on Sunday afternoon will sniff out a cynical "hit 'em where it hurts ploy." Then instead of the library being looked upon as an institution of integrity it will appear to be just another cynical, exploitive government entity. Libraries are best served by serving our patrons to the best of our ability with the resources at hand.[5]

Notes

1. Editorial, "Adopting Public Libraries," *Vindicator* (Youngstown, Ohio), July 16, 1996 (photocopy from the New York Public Library, Community Relations).

2. Commission on the Future of Libraries in Allegheny County, Pennsylvania, "The Knowledge Connection Program" (office memo), 1996, 6 pp.

3. David Scholz, "Feature Story," *The Business Journal* (Fresno, Calif.), April 29, 1996, quoted by Jean Saffell, Pub-Adv listserv, December 11, 1996.

4. American Library Association, Lib-Admin listserv, September 10, 1997.

5. "Libraries for the Future," Pub-Adv listserv October 2, 1997.

Chapter 40

Conclusion

How do libraries devise creative solutions? What plays into various approaches to benefit funding? The following points are distilled from the examples outlined in the previous chapter:

1. They find answers in *out of the way places,* in new constituencies, and in new organizations.
2. They find answers in *the community* and in *their profession.*
3. They look at *what is fundable* and design programs around it.
4. They look at the *unique characteristics* of their particular situation.
5. They *respond* when the community asks them to and then build on the response.
6. They have *"the guts to ask."*
7. They go to *extraordinary efforts* to make things work.
8. They *combine efforts.*
9. They keep *alert to possibilities* for their own involvement.
10. They tune in to *political and legal agendas.*
11. They look at *new solutions to old problems.*
12. They are *determined* to find solutions.

In short, "they leave no stones unturned." As a result, more stones are continually turning up.

RULE 7

RECAP

Chapter 41

Introduction

> Before I look at a library branch that I know I have assisted, and
> you are talking about over a million dollars, who is going to talk to
> me, who is going to show me what this million dollars is going to
> bring? How is this different to all of the projects that we have al-
> ready put in there?
>
> So, may I respectfully suggest that perhaps you not only provide
> that to me but you also provide all the resources that we have put
> into those libraries and see whether or not what was supposed to
> have happened happened. . . . I want to know what dollars that I put
> in got me in return.
>
> —Victor Robles, New York City Council member,
> "Transcript of the Minutes of the Preliminary Budget Hearing,"
> New York City, March 12, 1997, pp. 41–42

> After five years of extensive and sustained grassroots advocacy, we
> still don't formally evaluate other than to keep track of the total dol-
> lars added to the budget as a result of what we lobbied for.
>
> —Administrator of library Friends

> What gets measured gets done.
>
> —Attributed to Thomas J. Peters and Robert H. Waterman Jr.,
> *In Search of Excellence: Lessons from America's
> Best Run Companies* (New York: Harper & Row, 1982)

The following chapters take a look at library advocacy for funding purposes as a
professional initiative to be accommodated in the mainstream of library functions.
Two professional measurements are offered: an evaluation model applied to advocacy activities and a code of professional ethics for advocates.

Chapter 42

Evaluating Library Advocacy Efforts

Even library programs germane to public library services go along success-fully without ever being evaluated, so why should library advocacy, an upstart on the fringe of library practicum, merit the throes of an evaluation process? Why not capsulize advocacy evaluation with the query, Did we get what we asked for? This seems to be the view of library advocates. However, some jus-tification exists for evaluating advocacy efforts. A wide spectrum of advocacy efforts is under consideration—ranging from staff participation in community organizations to cost savings and superior public service—many of which were not implemented or were not performed for the purposes of advocacy so that, when used as tools of advocacy, they could warrant examination in this light. For example, libraries unable to get funding for their materials budgets from local public funders might redirect their energies to obtain private fund-ing for public Internet access. (Private funding for a novel idea is usually more easily obtainable than is funding for routine concerns.) Would public Internet access go on record as an advocacy effort? Hardly. However, in practice it is an advocacy effort because it not only results in immediate library funding but also can make the library more fundable in the future. Identifying the effort as such provides the opportunity to evaluate it for further benefit to future fund-ing.

Another reason for evaluating advocacy efforts is that many of these efforts do not produce funding results or influence for a long time, perhaps years (e.g., community activism and partnerships). The advocacy components of these ef-forts can consume a considerable amount of library staff time and funds for which accountability is in order. When expenditures of time and funds is sub-stantial, accountability can be on the firing line. If the adage "If something is worth doing, it's worth doing well" is applicable, then a standard must exist against which to measure doing something "well." To evaluate is to know what is being done in the first place to determine whether it is already being done well or whether intermediate steps are necessary before being done well is reached.

The support that public advocacy efforts give to the mission of the library being advocated is also important for evaluating advocacy efforts. For example, in its long-range plan of 1991–96, the Free Library of Philadelphia cites in support of its goal to provide outreach and promotional activities the objective "to develop and implement a plan to ensure effective community contacts in each public service area." Community contacts are the building blocks of library advocacy. Although advocacy is not mentioned per se, it is called into service to facilitate the library's mission. Evaluation would acknowledge this relationship and provide further clarification to the library's community emphasis.

The evaluation model presented in the next chapter provides library staff and other advocates with a simple way to track basic information to give reasonable consideration to the effort that they have spent many hours cultivating and expect to continue. Answers to the following questions are fundamental: Did the effort work? Did it do what we wanted it to do? Can the successes and failures be explained? Should we make changes? What other activities can we think up to meet our goals, given what we know about this one?

To answer these questions, the goals of the advocacy effort must first be clarified in terms of the library's mission and the purposes of the specific activities selected to meet those goals.

Assumptions and Goals

One way to define goals is by looking at the assumptions behind the efforts (emphasized in the discussions in this book) and then to generate goals from these assumptions. The key issues involved are the following:

- Quality service
- Accountability
- Communicating with the public

Assumptions

It is to the library's funding advantage that it does the following:

- *Provide outstanding public library service.* Public service is what the library is about. It must do its job well to gain the favor of its taxpayers.
- *Be accountable for the funds that it requests.* The library can expect continued funding only if it can show itself responsible for the funds that it already has received.
- *Provide the community with frequent and accurate information about library programs, activities, and services.* The library wants to attract

as many users in the community as possible to prove to funders that it is serving the community as it should.

- *Be familiar with local public funding officials and interact with them face to face for a variety of purposes.* To know public officials is to put library funding needs in the best light.
- *Consider new sources of funds.* To diversify funding shows responsible management, which influences the thinking of funders.
- *Form community partnerships.* Partnerships can provide funding solutions and a more efficient use of funds to impress funders.
- *Promote its resources as community assets.* The library can contribute positively to the community's economic base rather than be a cost center.
- *Listen and respond to community information needs.* The library is to be seen as a team player that facilitates community objectives.

Goals

To the end of fulfilling the previous objectives, the following goals for the library's advocacy efforts are defined:

Goal 1. The library's outstanding public service will be promoted to the community.

Goal 2. The library will be accountable to staff, customers, funders, and the community at large for the funds that it receives.

Goal 3. The library will provide the community with frequent and accurate information about library programs, activities, and services.

Goal 4. Library administration will be familiar with local public funding officials and interact with them directly and indirectly through written and verbal communication and face-to-face meetings.

Goal 5. The library will actively seek new funding sources.

Goal 6. The library will form community partnerships.

Goal 7. The library will promote its resources as community assets.

Goal 8. The library will solicit community input and respond to community information needs.

Given the goals of advocacy, the library can initiate activities that specifically support the goals or select library activities that are already up and running and focus on their advocacy component. For example, activities initiated or selected for each of the previous goals might be the following:

Goal 1: Public service. Activity: Local media ads

Goal 2: Accountability. Activity: Memoranda to city funders

Goal 3: Informing the community. Activity: A newsletter to library district residents

Goal 4: Meeting public officials. Activity: Team visits

Goal 5: New funding sources. Activity: Solicit corporate donations

Goal 6: Partnerships. Activity: Project cosponsorships with community organizations

Goal 7: Community assets. Activity: Promote job and career center

Goal 8: Community input. Activity: Appoint library staff representatives to
the community board

Focus for Evaluating

Which aspects to focus the evaluation on is another consideration when attempting to fulfill the goals that have been set. Some of the reasons for performing evaluations follow:

- To clarify what the library's advocacy efforts are
- To improve advocacy results
- To improve the advocacy process (the required time, effort, staffing, and funds)
- To justify future requests for funds that are specifically for advocacy ac-
tivities
- To generate more ideas for advocacy

From this information, the evaluation model is made to include the following points of focus:

- Identification of the activity
- Purpose in achieving the goal
- How the process of achieving the goal is implemented
- Time spent on achieving the goal
- Staffing
- Costs
- Source of funds
- Results
- Comments on other aspects for consideration
- Changes or additions to be implemented

Chapter 43

A Model: Summary Evaluations of a Hypothetical Library's Advocacy Activities

This chapter provides examples of summary evaluations (without the details) that are based on actual or prospective advocacy efforts as reported by library administrators. These examples illustrate a range of activities on behalf of library advocacy.

Exhibit 1

Goal 1. The library's outstanding public service will be promoted to the community.

Activity: Three sixty-second infomercials for local cable television

Purpose: To identify the library with excellent public service among general audiences and to "advertise" its services to attract customers

Implementation: Library Friends project under the direction of a local public relations consultant; run for one month several times weekly on cable television

Staffing: Friends

Costs: $6,500 to design and produce

Funding source: All costs donated by Friends

Results: Positive feedback from library users who were surprised to learn that we could provide certain kinds of reference services and information; 10 percent increase in phone queries at reference desk during the time period the infomercials ran; 2 percent increase in new card holders at this time

Comments: Local council members were sent copies of the videos; no response to date

Changes or additions: Friends will look into measuring cost-benefit ratios for the possibility of soliciting outside funds to produce and distribute additional videos and infomercials

Date: Completed by: Reviewed by:

Exhibit 2

Goal 2. The library will make clear its mission and intentions—and its fulfillment of these to staff, customers, funders, and the community at large—to comply with its commitment to accountability for the funds that it receives.

Activity: Periodic memoranda to city funders with details of how public funds were used and who benefited from those funds and a progress update on relevant projects

Purpose: To reinforce our commitment in the minds of public funders

Implementation: Reminders to staff at monthly branch meetings in a standardized format and mailed to council members (names) in branch library districts (names), on January 1, May 15, and September 8

Staffing: Managers of appropriate branch libraries (names) and library director (name)

Costs: Staff hours—2 at an estimated $20 per hour, or $40 per memo

Funding source: General operating

Results: Council member (name) acknowledged in budget hearing; council member (name) cited in press statement; funding approved for current fiscal year

Comments:

Changes or additions: File reports at front desk for public use; cite on Web page; keep to one-page limit

Date: Completed by: Reviewed by:

Exhibit 3

Goal 3. The library will provide the community with frequent and accurate information about library programs, activities, and services.

Activity: Four-page monthly newsletter mailed to all library district residences (ten issues per year)

Purpose: To keep our constituents aware of the library and what it is doing for their benefit

Implementation: Editorial board meets monthly to decide what to include: what is essential to report on; which programs are offered; how programs, activities, and services affect the community; and what to provide reminders about

Staffing: Editorial board—director, assistant director, and community service librarian; two volunteers do the mailing

Costs: $3,500 production and mailing budget for 5,000 copies. Staff time—average 8 hours for each of 3 staff members 10 times per year for a total of 240 hours at an average of $20 per hour for a total labor cost of $4,800

Funding source: Operating budget

Results: Library users mention newsletter frequently; it seems to be working as an information tool

Comments: The light humor seems especially appealing to users

Changes or additions: Consider a questions-and-answers column about the library to get more input from the community (in addition to the question box we already use)

Date: Completed by: Reviewed by:

Exhibit 4

Goal 4. Library administration will become familiar with local public funding officials and interact with them through written and verbal communication and face-to-face meetings.

Activity: Team visits to city council members, county officials, and mayor

Purpose: To keep the library's cause fresh in the council's mind so that they acknowledge their responsibility for library building maintenance, to show our continued appreciation for the five-year funding agreement with the county, and to keep the mayor informed

Implementation: We assigned twenty-one two- and three-member teams of staff, trustees, and Friends (one each when possible); each visited a different official and reported to a team coordinator (see details of assignments attached)

Staffing: Volunteers: 19 Friends, 10 trustees, 26 library staff at an estimated 6 hours per person (55) for 3 visits, or 330 hours

Supplies: Stationery and postage for follow-up letters (under $20)

Costs: Time and supplies donated

Funding source: Friends

Results: Visits to twelve county officials, the mayor, and eight city council members; all city council members visited except the council chair, who refused to see us but said that he would vote for the library; officials listened attentively and asked only a few questions (some took notes or had an assistant take notes); all seemed to appreciate our efforts; the city voted funds for building maintenance (an improvement over the previous year, when the city would not vote any funds for capital expenses)

Comments: We asked team leaders to try hard to get their public officials into the library (five of them were successful); we explained to the council chair that it was not just his vote we wanted but that we wanted all members to be better informed about the library; attendance at training session was poor—how can it be improved next year?

Date: Completed by: Reviewed by:

Exhibit 5

Goal 5. The library will actively seek new funding sources.

Activity: Solicited community businesses to fund local business archives startup

Purpose: To get local business on our side as a funding partner on a continuing basis to fund the library's new business archives

Implementation: Library director and staff representative to the Chamber of Commerce announced the project at a Chamber meeting; several businesses volunteered support; trustees also helped get contributions

Staffing: Library director, development director, and volunteers (trustees)

Time and costs: Library director's time—16 hours at $30 per hour, or $480; development director—20 hours at $20 per hour, or $400; total $880

Funding source: Miscellaneous fees

Results: Income—$10,000 total from twenty local business donors

Comments: Donors are enthusiastic; some want to contribute company materials to archives

Changes or additions: Director will try to get more trustees to participate

Date: Completed by: Reviewed by:

Exhibit 6

Goal 6. The library will form community partnerships.

Activity: Library worked with the Rotary Club and the Downtown Development Association to plan and install a garden and outdoor reading area adjacent to the library

Purpose: To prove the library's effectiveness as a partner with community organizations that are in a position to fund future library programs and to have major input into an enhancement to the library

Implementation: Planning discussions and contracts with outside vendors

Staffing: Director took part in planning discussions and helped review credentials of prospective contractors

Costs and time: Director's time—about 4 hours monthly for 12 months, or 48 hours at $31 per hour, or $4,188

Funding source: General operating (director's salary)

Results: Project moving ahead as planned to date (Rotary has expressed interest in funding the library's literacy project)

Comments: Project came about as a result of director's participation in the Rotary for three years and as a board member for two years

Additions or changes: Provide project description to Rotary for literacy project

Date: Completed by: Reviewed by:

Exhibit 7

Goal 7. The library will promote its resources as community assets.

Activity: Promote job and career center

Purpose: To let local funders know how the library is helping job seekers get jobs

Implementation: Kept records for one year on materials usage, demographics of users (including jobs held), follow-ups regarding success of job search, and user evaluations of job center's services; success rates compared favorably to those of a similar labor department project two years ago; prepared three-page executive summary report and press release and sent report to public funding officials

Staffing: Job center director with Ph.D. student in public affairs (volunteer)

Costs and time: Director of job center—2 days per month, or 24 per year, at $16 per hour, or $384

Funding source: General operating funds, per salary

Results: Public officials acknowledged receipt of report and are considering funding an increase in the job center's budget for the next fiscal year; the city's largest newspaper carried a story about the center based on our press release; use of the center increased 10 percent immediately following the story; numbers are holding

Comments: Follow up with public officials

Changes or additions: Send press releases to community newspapers

Date: Completed by: Reviewed by:

Exhibit 8

Goal 8. The library will solicit community input and respond to community information needs.

Activity: Library sent a representative to the local community board in the library's district

Purpose: To be aware of the needs of other community organizations that might generate new or cooperative library services and to use this vehicle to dispense library news for possible funding advantage

Implementation: Community services staff member, assistant, or both attend board meetings and relevant committee meetings monthly and then report by interoffice memo to library director any news of potential interest for library development

Staffing: Community services staff

Costs and time: Representatives attend meetings on their own time

Funding source: Per salary, time equivalent

Results: We were able to get board members to advocate for an increase in the library's materials budget at library budget hearings (increase was approved); have added new materials for immigrants as a result of information from a community service organization and a member of the community board that serves recent immigrants

Comments: Community boards help us facilitate other connections

Additions or changes: Should we alternate staff representatives?

Date: Completed by: Reviewed by:

What the Evaluations Do

These evaluations offer several outcomes:

1. Focus the thinking of administrators, board members, and advocates on the activities that benefit advocacy and why they benefit that advocacy
2. Measure the usefulness of certain library activities
3. Identify the need for more specific information and measurements
4. Help clarify the goals of the library's advocacy efforts in terms of the library's mission
5. Describe the library's performance to library funding and other interests outside the library
6. Provide a reference for planning future advocacy efforts
7. Demonstrate the library's commitment to effectiveness

In summary, these evaluations spotlight the library's advocacy efforts in terms of the library's total functioning. This is appropriate because the library is made possible only with the necessary funding—and funding is the goal of advocacy. Here we are again, back at square one.

Chapter 44

Ethical and Legal Considerations of Public Library Advocacy

Ethical considerations involve questions of morality, integrity, and professional standards and probably have about the same degree of impact on the practice of most of the public library advocacy discussed in this book as they do on other library activities in which personal interaction is primary (e.g., reference service). That is, the impact of ethical considerations, or the lack thereof, on advocacy efforts might be of some consequence, but probably not considerably so. However, when advocacy moves into the area of private fund-raising, where library staff are accountable for major personal gifts received or might be privy to confidential information regarding personal wealth, ethical issues are more likely to come to the fore. This issue has been addressed in depth in the literature of fund-raising for nonprofit organizations.

If the stock in trade of fund-raising is money, that of advocacy is action. Because actions of misbehavior—as long as money is not at issue—do not ordinarily cause problems of the dimension that misuses of money do (this might be arguable), it would seem practical to focus ethical considerations for public library advocacy on professional standards and leave everyone to handle for themselves the finer points of morality and integrity that can affect professional standards. Referring to the American Library Association's (ALA's) code of ethics, which emphasizes mainly professional standards, ethics and integrity are inferred by the use of such value words as *outstanding* and *highest,* which leave room for interpretation by one's own value system. However, without further explanation, the code does put those for whom the code is intended on notice that their actions may be subject to professional and ethical review. Other wording implanted in the code might be inspired by activities of the opposite bent that were known to have caused trouble in the past, for example, *accurate*), where inaccuracies of information have been rampant, or *commitment,* where a lack of such has been an egregious shortfall. (Perhaps it is possible to read the history of an organization's professional conduct in its most recent ethics code!)

The following code of ethics for advocates is based on the goals of advocacy presented earlier in the previous chapter. In terms of ethical implications, the key issues are disclosure, accountability, and community responsibility.

The first three goals and the eighth goal outlined in the previous chapter (pertaining to public service, accountability, and community relations) have ethical overtones in their focus on personal and financial relationships and therefore lend themselves to inclusion in adopting the code. In addition, because the history of advocacy has squared off on occasion with the legal profession, legal issues are also referred to in the code.

The library's mission is number one in the code. Considering that many library advocates are not library staff but Friends, trustees, and others in the neighborhood, this could be an important part of the advocacy code, requiring occasional review by advocates and clarification by library administration. In some cases, library advocates have decided the library should be something that it is not or should be situated somewhere that it has no intention of being and then base their advocacy on these assumptions, with disastrous results. A rural Pennsylvania county attributed its loss of a referendum to this reason. Therefore, faithfulness to the library's mission takes first place in the code, as follows.

Advocacy Code of Ethics for Library Staff and Other Advocates

Whereas the library's actions and accountability for funds entrusted with us are instrumental in influencing the library's public and private funders to respond favorably to our funding requests,

1. We will base our advocacy efforts on the mission and goals of the library for which we are advocating.
2. We will provide the public with outstanding service, whether for the use of library resources or to obtain public information on library management and policies, knowing that as a public institution we are answerable to our taxpayers.
3. We will make clear the library's mission and intentions, and their fulfillment or reasons for lack of fulfillment, to staff, customers, funders, and the community at large in compliance with our commitment to accountability for public and private funds received.
4. We will provide the library community with frequent and accurate information about library programs, activities, and services that these might benefit the greatest number of persons in the library's service area and especially those for whom the program, activity, or service is most relevant.

5. We will take into account the needs of other community organizations as ascertained from our networking activities and other means of communication in formulating our requests for library funds.
6. We will comply to the best of our ability with federal and local laws that govern public advocacy efforts.

The most important legal concern for libraries and other organizations involved in advocacy is in the issue of lobbying, which applies to nonprofit organizations and has specific rules of legality attached to it. Lobbying is a form of advocacy that promotes a particular candidate for office and that library advocates are usually careful to avoid, concentrating their political efforts instead on promoting the library's interests—programs, activities, and budget—for the purpose of information and education. State and local restrictions exist as well on lobbying activities that might apply to a specific library.

Shared with the ALA's ethics code of 1995 is a commitment to public service, which is the foundation of public library operations and which advocates also consider the foremost component of public library advocacy. Two words stand out that especially distinguish the advocate's code from that of the ALA: *community*, referring to the fact that advocacy is a community-oriented initiative, and *accountability*, referring to its relationship to funding. These differences, and the fact that library advocacy is firmly entrenched as a public library initiative, invite the possibility of expanding the ALA's code to accommodate library advocacy efforts.

Chapter 45

Conclusion

The previous chapters have considered a model evaluation of advocacy efforts and the development of an advocates code of ethics, giving representative examples of each. These activities are geared to treating public library advocacy as a legitimate and central endeavor in today's libraries. The model documents are intended for professional review and dialogue to make them useful in the missions of specific libraries and to enhance the standards of the library profession at large.

RULE 8

IN CONCLUSION

Chapter 46

Advocacy into the Future

The discussion in this book has focused on public library advocacy for funding purposes. To do so, it has presented a rather skewed version of a public library, one in which the name of the game is funding. Most people realize that libraries have greater missions than to be funded. These missions—to make available whatever forms of information and services are considered by the profession to be within the legally, ethically, and professionally correct functions of a public library—are discussed in many eminent publications with no concern for their funding suitability. Nor should there be such concern.

However, this book's purpose is to illustrate various library activities with a view to their "fundability." The politics of funding is a reality of the times and most often an important consideration in managing a public library. It can challenge traditional structures and practices so that the library becomes a different entity that affects how things are done—which programs and services are emphasized and which are withdrawn regardless of certain values they might offer. Library directors might now spend more than half their time in funding concerns while collection development and programs lag. Even library Friends groups, originally organized for the purpose of book and author luncheons, now scramble to put together team visits to local elected officials. Funding is one of the most important considerations facing public libraries today, if not the most important, and it colors the way in which things are done and the relationships that ensue.

Of course, downsides to this state of the art do exist, but this book is about the upsides, namely, that the skills and forms that advocacy has generated to serve funding needs—skills such as deciphering community needs, looking at the library from a community perspective, talking assets, costing out benefits, emphasizing accountability, and forms such as teams and partnerships—will not only be central in the continued negotiating of public library budgets but will also provide the path to solving other library concerns—of identity, image, relations with community power centers, and the relevancy of the library to its users—that dominate library professional discussions and Internet listservs. Of the various tools and strategies, forms, and practices of public library advocacy referred to in this book, partnerships seem to be the most important with their implications for the long term. When a library becomes a partner, it is no longer the same organization that it was. It takes on new roles and identities not only as a result of the partnership's goals but also as a result of the process of working together and arriving at those goals. Traditional values of library management take second place at that point to the need for the success of the partnership with an eye to its reverberations in the community, for a library to take on even the most modest of partnerships is to expand its thinking to accommodate the thinking of its partners, and doing so opens a window to change.

Partnerships born in library advocacy, together with library information systems, indicate dynamic restructuring of libraries and implications for their future funding. The influx of library information systems has brought to the forefront the public library's two-allegiance encampment. One allegiance is to those who require specific information with little regard for the format in which it is delivered, such as students, researchers, business, government, and community organizations. The other allegiance is to those for whom formats are at least as important as the information relayed. These are children, teenagers, seniors, nonreaders, immigrants, neighborhood schmoozers, and so on, who favor picture books, large-print type, video- and audiotapes, instructional materials, newspapers, and magazines. Whereas information is the banner for the first camp, goodwill is that for the second.

The two camps—call them Camp Info and Camp Goodwill—have different funding postures. Camp Goodwill has the advantage of attracting local elected officials who need to solve community economic and social problems and, through the efforts of library advocates, are alerted to the library's ability to help reach these objectives. Camp Info has less obvious goals that are more inherent to the role that information access plays in building the infrastructure of a democratic society—concepts hard to pin down and not capable of mixing very well with the exigencies of local political agendas.

As a result, different funding solutions might be in order. Camp Info might increasingly look to larger units of funding (regional and national) that support the collaborative information access required by this camp, whereas Camp Goodwill remains keyed in to local funding sources that support the community's welfare.

What this portends is the restructuring of public libraries as the information partnerships result in new entities and certain technical functions spin off in new directions. It is not the purpose of this book's conclusion to predict where the public library is going—only that the advocacy skills and forms that have risen out of funding needs are the tools that are going to take it there. In the process of advocacy, libraries have honed new allegiances, and it is these that will determine the nature of the public libraries of the twenty-first century.

APPENDIXES

Appendix 1

Checklist of Advocates, Forms, and Funders

Library Advocates

Library director
Library administrative staff
Library board members
Other librarians
Other staff
Library association staff
Library users
Volunteers
Library Friends
Business owners
Other community representatives

Funders and Agents

Public officials
Community foundations
Library foundations
Corporations
Corporate foundations
Library users

Types of Funds

Public funds
Private funds

Capital funds
Operating funds

Forms of Library Advocacy

Internal Operations

Public service
Community surveys
Community input
Asset management
Diversified funding
Leveraging funds
Leveraging resources
Cost-benefit analyses
Cost-saving initiatives
Team efforts
Staff training
New stakeholders
New buildings
New technologies
User statistics
Long-range planning
Evaluations

External Operations

Partnerships
Formal agreements
Customized programs
Advertising and marketing
Public relations
Community activism
Media coverage
Newsletters
Referendum campaigns
Community meetings
Minding the opposition
Demonstrating accountability
Letters to public officials
Ongoing relations with public officials
Hosting public officials
Visits to public officials
Budget action

Appendix 2

Examples of Advocacy Documents

15. Referendum campaigns—"Look at Brooks," Friends of Brooks Free Library (p. 196)
16. Ongoing relations with public officials—Excerpt from *Budget Action Handbook,* New York Public Library (p. 198)
17. Visits to public officials—"Informational visits to elected officials' offices," excerpt from *Budget Action Handbook,* New York Public Library (p. 200)
18. Budget action—"Expansion Budget Passes!" (newsletter), Floyd Memorial Library (p. 202)
19. Budget action—"Save Public Libraries," Friends of the Prince George's County Libraries (p. 203)
20. Budget action—"Budget Action Components," excerpt from *Budget Action Handbook,* New York Public Library (p. 204)
21. Budget action—"Statement of New York City FY 1995 Expense Priorities," excerpt from *Budget Action Handbook,* New York Public Library (p. 205)
22. "Drop Everything and Write . . ." (flyer), New York Public Library (p. 206)
23. "Log-on," American Library Association (ALA) (p. 207)

The Power of Suggestion

The Rochester Hills Public Library always welcomes compliments, concerns, and suggestions from anyone who uses the library. Each form put in the suggestion box at the Information Desk is carefully reviewed by library director Christine Hage. Thank you for caring enough about the library to help us improve, keep up the good work, or see something from a different perspective. You may wish to mail this card (be sure to affix postage).

_____

_____

_____

_____

_____

_____

_____

_____

OPTIONAL

From: _____ Date: _____ Please contact me at: _____

KOKOMO-HOWARD COUNTY PUBLIC LIBRARY
ART COLLECTION POLICY

PHILOSOPHY
The Kokomo-Howard County Public Library accepts, as part of its mission to provide expertly selected materials which aid the individual in the pursuit of education, information or research and the creative use of leisure time, the collection of works of art for display in the library.

SCOPE OF COLLECTION
It shall be the policy of the library to collect pieces of art that are by artists affiliated with the State of Indiana or that depict Indiana scenes, in general, and within that framework to also purchase those pieces by local artists which meet the guidelines of the collection.

GUIDELINES FOR COLLECTION BUILDING
To reflect the auxiliary nature of an art collection to the library's mission, a maximum size for the collection shall be placed at 200 pieces.

The purchase of pieces for the collection shall be limited to an average of two per year, with funds from the Gift and Memorials Fund.

Purchases shall be limited to two-dimensional art due to the special problems of holding three-dimensional pieces.

The content of the collection shall be assessed periodically by a knowledgeable person to help determine strengths and weaknesses, with the intent of using that information to maintain a strong collection through carefully selected additions and withdrawals.

ACQUISITIONS
The library director will obtain permission from the library board before purchasing any additions to the Hoosier Art Collection. If the board desires, and if it is feasible, the board may take the opportunity to look at a work of art or a photograph thereof and compare it to one or two other works that are similar before approving the purchase of a new work of art.

Prior to a decision to purchase a work of art, at least two knowledgeable people will have been asked to comment on it. This information will be shared with the appropriate library representatives. Also, an opinion concerning the value of the work of art will be obtained from at least one reputable source other than the seller.

GIFTS

The library's Artwork Donation Policy shall govern the acceptance of pieces of art. Artwork will be accepted for inclusion in the collection if it meets the guidelines for collection building.

ORGANIZATION

Careful documentation shall be maintained of pertinent information about the artist and the work of art, consistent with the philosophy and purpose of the collection.

A photo collection shall be established and maintained to form archival documentation of the works held.

CONSERVATION

To ensure that individual pieces are maintained at a standard consistent with the most effective use of the collection, cleaning and repair shall be provided as needed. Funding for this maintenance shall be from the Gift and Memorial Fund.

DISPLAY

To ensure maximum benefit from the collection for the library's patrons, shows shall be hung at least twice per year, with appropriate educational emphasis and artist and item identification.

Adopted June 1989
Revised March 1991

Cumberland County Library System

LIBRARY SERVICE VALUE

With a $2.2 million budget, the library system provided more than $34 million worth of great services. In effect, it multiplied the community's dollars more than 15 times!

Books
Borrowed 1,228,083 times.
If people had purchased the books
at $25 each:..........................$30,702,075

Books-on-Tape
Borrowed 113,831 times.
If people had purchased the tapes
at $20 each:............................$2,276,620

Video Cassettes
Borrowed 131,201 times.
If people had rented the tapes
at $3 each:................................$393,603

Magazines
Borrowed 33,820 times.
If people had purchased the
magazines at $3 each:...
....$101,460

Programs
38,959 People Attended 1,662
Children's & Adult Programs.
If people had paid $5 each:...
....$194,795

Reference Questions
Librarians answered 41,381
questions.
If people had paid $10 for each
answer:......................................$413,810

STAR (Service to Adult Readers)
12,927 items delivered to homebound
and facilities.
If people had paid $25 for each large
print book or books-on-tape:...
....$323,175

LIBRARY SERVICE VALUE:
$34,405,538

Brooklyn Public Library
BUSINESS LIBRARY
280 Cadman Plaza West
Brooklyn, NY 11201

718/722-3333   Fax 718/722-3337
LAN ACCESS # 718/797-4973

1997 FACT SHEET

1. BUILDING (Brooklyn Heights Branch and Business Library)
Renovation started..........................December 16, 1991
Opened to the public........................October 12, 1993
Architect................David Prendergast & Associates
Size of building...62,000 square feet (4 levels: 2 stories, 2 basement floors)
Book capacity.......open shelf capacity: 86,000 volumes
closed stacks and storage: 239,200 volumes
Auditorium .... Seats 134
Brooklyn Heights Branch....accommodates 140 patrons
Business Library...............accommodates 140 patrons

2. HISTORY OF BUSINESS LIBRARY
Founded...1943
Located at 197 Montague St. (in same building as
Montague Branch) 1943-1961
Temporary quarters (141 Livingston St.)...1961-May 1962
Located at 280 Cadman Plaza West (in same building
as the renamed community library, Brooklyn
Heights Branch)........June 1962-August 1991
Temporary quarters (148 Pierrepont St.)...August 1991-
October 1993

3. HOURS OF SERVICE
Monday..10-8
Tuesday...1-8
Wednesday..10-6
Thursday..1-6
Friday..10-6
Saturday..10-5
Hours may vary.

4. STAFF
11 Librarians
9 Appointed clerks
6 Part-timers
1 Outreach Specialist

5. EQUIPMENT AND MACHINES
2 Microfilm readers
1 Microfilm/fiche
reader/printer
10 Microfilm reader-printers
1 Microcard reader
4 Microfiche readers
5 Microfiche reader-printers
5 Photocopy machines
1 Fax machine
16 Computers with CD-ROM drives and printers

Photocopies made from film and microfiche (1996): 41,937

6. BOOK STOCK (as of January 1, 1997)
Reference books.......................................102,003
Circulating books..30,987
Total..132,990

7. NONBOOK STOCK (as of January 1, 1997)
Reels of microfilm.......................................19,332
Microfiche..728,892
Microcard..30,000
CD ROM titles..84
CD ROM disks...1,682

8. SERIALS (as of January 1, 1997)
Periodical subscriptions.................................1,435
Newspapers...20
Total..1,455

Directories
United States...665
Foreign..540
Service..1,127
Product..530
Total..2,862

U.S. Government publications
(open entries)...1,000

Serials (exclusive of U.S.)...............................2,000

Telephone books
New York State..270
United States cities (on microfiche).............847
Foreign..355
Total..1,472

9. READER STATISTICS (1996)
Call slips...6,556
Information and ready reference....................52,107
Reference...83,453
Telephone calls...35,901

10. PUBLICATIONS
Business Rankings Annual, in conjunction with Gale
Research

11. FURTHER READINGS
Investment Dealers' Digest, April 15, 1975, pages 28-29
New York Times, May 4, 1975, Sect. III, page 4
Free Enterprise, February 1978, pages 46-48
Daily News, December 31, 1982, page 28
New York City Business, March 26, 1984, pages 22-23
The Phoenix, Part 2, December 17, 1987, page 11
Bookmark, Fall 1988, page 17
New York Newsday, Brooklyn Section, December 8, 1991, pages 2-3
Daily News, Brooklyn Section, October 10, 1993, page 1
Crain's New York Business, January 23, 1995, page 20

January 1997

THE FRIENDS
of the
SAINT PAUL
PUBLIC LIBRARY

September 3, 1996

Ms. Carolyn H. Roby
Program Director
Norwest Corporation
Norwest Foundation
Norwest Center, 6th & Marquette
Minneapolis, MN 55479-1055

Dear Carolyn:

The Friends of the Saint Paul Public Library is a 51 year old private nonprofit organization whose purpose is to support the Saint Paul Public Library. The Friends supports the Library through fundraising activities, advocacy efforts and adult programming. The mission statement for The Friends of the Saint Paul Public Library is as follows:

The Friends of the Saint Paul Public Library supports the Saint Paul Public Library and helps the Library expand its potential to serve the Saint Paul community. In supporting the Library, The Friends will involve the community by:

- Stimulating interest in and use of the Saint Paul Public Library;

- Raising funds in a manner which does not diminish the need for strong public funding of the Library; and

- Acting as an advocate for the Library.

For the last year, The Friends and the Saint Paul Public Library have worked closely with four small business assistance programs in the Twin Cities metropolitan area. As a result of this series of meetings during this last year, The Friends and the Library are requesting that Norwest Foundation support an innovative project which emerged from this planning process. We are requesting a multi-year grant in the amount of $194,550 to be awarded in installments over a three year period.

The project being proposed here would electronically link four small business assistance providers (WomenVenture, Neighborhood Development Center, Metropolitan Economic Development Association and the Small Business Development Center at the University of Saint Thomas) with the Saint Paul Public Library. These small business assistance providers would then have access to all of the materials which would be available at the Library to assist entrepreneurs in the development and growth of a small business.

The funding requested would purchase dedicated workstations for each small business assistance program to access the Library's materials. Funds would also pay for a staff coordinator position to implement this project, technical assistance for problems associated with this new technology and new reference materials to supplement what is currently available at the Saint Paul Public Library.

This project is a perfect fit for Norwest Foundation's corporate giving guidelines in the category of economic improvement for adults and families. It assists with management training, financial counseling and job seeking skill development. Furthermore, this project creates new and on-going linkages between some of the major small business assistance providers in the Twin Cities and one of the largest reference libraries in the state.

This project is one of a number of projects which have come from a long range planning process on the part of the Library. This planning process has led to the creation of a capital campaign intended to raise private and public funds for a number of Library projects over the next three years. This project comprises one component of the overall capital campaign for which fundraising has just begun.

Thank you for your serious consideration of this funding request. If you have any additional questions, please feel free to call me or any of the other partners involved in this model project.

Sincerely,

Peter D. Pearson
Executive Director

PAUL VARACALLI
Executive Director
MARGARET BUTZ SHELLEDA
Deputy Executive Director
522 Grand Avenue
Oakland, CA 94610-3599
Phone (510) 465-0120
FAX (510) 451-6928
1390 Market Street
Suite 1118
San Francisco, CA 94102-5305
Phone (415) 575-1740
FAX (415) 431-6241

February 2, 1994

Save Our Library

TO: All Oakland Library Chapter Members

Is $20 a worthwhile investment to save Library jobs and improve book collections and programs?

We are asking each Library member for a pledge of financial support for the June ballot measure that would, if passed, provide a permanent source of funding for the Oakland Public Library. The source would be a parcel tax of under $50 per household.

The most valuable financial support for any ballot measure is early support. We can use your early contribution for mailings and events that will raise more money to pass the measure. That's why we are asking you to contribute now.

Please fill out the coupon below and return it with your check (payable to "Save Our Library") to Brad Walters, Circulation Desk, Main Library, or one of the other Library Stewards.

Let's have 100% support from LocaL 790 members! Thank you!

Brad Walters, Chief Steward   Margaret Cunningham, Field Rep

Here is my contribution to the "Save Our Library" campaign:

____$20 or more (Librarians)

____$15 or more (PT Librarians, Library Assistants)

____$10 or more (PT Library Assistants, Library Aides)

Name_____ Work Site_____

Current Address_____

Home Telephone Number_____

CITY OF PALM SPRINGS

CONTRACT SERVICES AGREEMENT FOR

MUNICIPAL PUBLIC LIBRARY SERVICES

THIS CONTRACT SERVICES AGREEMENT (herein "Agreement") is made and entered into this second (2nd) day of October, 1996, by and between the City of Palm Springs, a municipal corporation (herein "City") and City of Palm Springs Board of Library Trustees. (herein "Contractor").

NOW, THEREFORE, the parties hereto agree as follows:

1.0 SERVICES OF CONTRACTOR

1.1 Scope of Services. In compliance with all of the terms and conditions of this Agreement, the Contractor shall perform the work or services set forth in the "Scope of Services" attached hereto as Exhibit "A" and incorporated herein by reference. Contractor warrants that all work and services set forth in the Scope and Services will be performed in a competent, professional and satisfactory manner.

1.2 Compliance With Law. All work and services rendered hereunder shall be provided in accordance with all ordinances, resolutions, statutes, rules, and regulations of the City and any Federal, State or local governmental agency of competent jurisdiction.

1.3 Licenses, Permits, Fees and Assessments. Contractor shall obtain at its sole cost and expense such licenses as may be required by law for the performance of the services required by this Agreement. Required permits under the control of the City shall be granted to the Contractor at no cost but subject to normal approval policies and procedures of the City. Fees and assessments under the control of the City shall also be waived.

2.0 COMPENSATION

2.1 Contract Sum. For the services rendered pursuant to this Agreement, Contractor shall be compensated in accordance with the "Schedule of Compensation" attached hereto as Exhibit "B" and incorporated herein by this reference. In addition, the Contractor maintains a Library Trust Fund ("Trust Fund") which provides additional funding to supplement and enrich the the quality of the public library. All donations, fines, fees, Library Center room rental receipts and state public library subventions shall supplement the compensation defined in Exhibit "B" and be placed into the "Trust Fund."

3.0 COORDINATION OF WORK

3.1 Representative of Contractor. The City Librarian is hereby designated as being the principal and representative of Contractor authorized to act in its behalf with respect to the work and services specified herein and make all decisions in connection therewith.

3.2 Contract Officer. The City Manager is hereby designated as being the representative the City authorized to act in its behalf with respect to the work and services specified herein and make all decisions in connection therewith ("Contract Officer"). The City Manager of City shall have the right to designate another Contract Officer by providing written notice to Contractor.

3.3 Prohibition Against Subcontracting or Assignment. Contractor shall not contract with any entity to perform in whole or in part the work or services required hereunder without the express written approval of the City. Neither this Agreement nor any interest herein may be assigned or transferred,voluntarily or by operation of law, without the prior written approval of City. Any such prohibited assignment or transfer shall be void.

3.4 Independent Contractor. The Board of Library Trustees shall retain its authority under the California Education Code and City Charter as an independent legal entity. Contractor shall perform all services required hereunder as an independent contractor of City such that the City shall have no control over the manner, mode or means by which Contractor performs services and Contractor shall have only such obligations as are consistent with its role as an independent contractor. Said Board shall continue to be appointed by the City Council subject to the provisions delineated under the California Education Code (Sections 18900-18965) as amended.

Notwithstanding, the above, under the provisions of this Agreement, the City Librarian and the library staff shall remain employees of the City of Palm Springs subject to the same benefits, controls and disciplinary actions applicable to other City employees of similar classification. The City Librarian shall remain a department head with a reporting responsibility to both the City Manager and the Board of Library Trustees.

4.0 INSURANCE AND INDEMNIFICATION

4.1 Insurance and Indemnification. Under the terms of this Agreement, the Library Center, historical museums (Exhibit A, item "6") and the former Crocker branch library shall remain property of the City of Palm Springs and shall be insured under said City's insurance policies. Library Trustees, employees and volunteers shall continue to be indemnified by the City to the same extent as commissioners, staff and volunteers of other City departments.

5.0 TERM

5.1 <u>Term</u>. Unless earlier terminated in accordance with Section 5.2 below, this Agreement shall continue in full force and effect until June 30, 2001.

5.2 <u>Termination Prior to Expiration of Term</u>. Either party may terminate this Agreement at the conclusion of any fiscal year (June 30) within the term stated above. However, such termination will require at least four (4) votes on the part of either the Palm Springs City Council or the Library Board at least thirty (30) days prior to the proposed termination date. In the event of said termination the funding and management of the City's public library services will revert to the extant municipal budget and management policies.

6.0 MISCELLANEOUS

6.1 <u>Covenant Against Discrimination</u>. Contractor covenants that, by and for itself, its heirs, executors, assigns and all persons claiming under or through them, that there shall be no discrimination against or segregation of, any person or group of persons on account of race, color, creed, religion, sex, marital status, national origin, or ancestry in the performance of this Agreement. Contractor shall take affirmative action to ensure that applicants are employed and that employees are treated during employment without regard to their race, color, creed, religion, sex, marital status, national origin or ancestry.

6.2 <u>Notice</u>. Any notice, demand, request, document, consent, approval, or communication either party desires or is required to give to the other party or any other person shall be in writing and either served personally or sent by prepaid, first-class mail, in the case of the City, to the City Manager and to the attention of the Contract Officer, CITY OF PALM SPRINGS, P. O. Box 2743, Palm Springs, California 92263, and in the case of the Contractor, to the person at the address designated on the execution page of this Agreement.

6.3 <u>Interpretation.</u> The terms of this Agreement shall be construed in accordance with the meaning of the language used and shall not be construed for or against either party by reason of the authoship of this Agreement or any other rule of construction which might otherwise apply.

6.4   Integration; Amendment. It is understood that there are no oral agreements between the parties hereto affecting this Agreement and this Agreement supersedes and cancels any and all previous negotiations, arrangements, agreements and understandings, if any, between the parties, and none shall be used to interpret this Agreement. This Agreement may be amended at any time by the mutual consent of the parties by an instrument in writing.

6.5   Severability. In the event that part of this Agreement shall be declared invalid or unenforceable by a valid judgment or decree of a court of competent jurisdiction, such invalidity or unenforceability shall not affect any of the remaining portions of this Agreement which are hereby declared as severable and shall be interpreted to carry out the intent of the parties hereunder unless the invalid provision is so material that its invalidity deprives either party of the basic benefit of their bargain or renders this Agreement meaningless.

6.6   Waiver. No delay or omission in the exercise of any right or remedy by a nondefaulting party on any default shall impair such right or remedy or be construed as a waiver. A party's consent to or approval of any act by the other party requiring the party's consent or approval shall not be deemed to waive or render unecessary the other party's consent to or approval of any subsequent act. Any waiver by either party of any defaut must be in writing and shall not be a waiver of any other default concerning the same or any other provision of this Agreement.

6.7   Attorney's Fees. The Board of Library Trustees, City Librarian, library staff and library volunteers shall remain agents of the City of Palm Springs under the terms of this Agreement and therefore subject to the same legal defense and reimbursement for legal fees as commissions, staff and volunteers of other City departments.

6.8   Authority. The persons executing this Agreement on behalf of the parties hereto warrant that (i) such party is duly organized and existing, (ii) they are duly authorized to execute and deliver this Agreement on behalf of said party, (iii) by so executing this Agreement, such party is formally bound to the provisions of this Agreement, and (iv) the entering into this Agreement does not violate any provision of any other Agreement to which said party is bound.

IN WITNESS WHEREOF, the parties have executed and entered into this Agreement as of the date first written above.

CITY:
CITY OF PALM SPRINGS
a municipal corporation

ATTEST:

_____

City Manager

_____

CITY OF PALM SPRINGS (City Clerk area)

CONTRACTOR:

City Clerk

_____

APPROVED AS TO FORM: _____

_____   By:_____

City Attorney   Name:
Title:

EXHIBIT "A"

<u>SCOPE OF SERVICES</u>

In exchange for the contract allocations described in "Schedule B" of this Agreement, the contractor (Board of Library Trustees) commits to providing at least the following levels of public library services for the residents and visitors of the City of Palm Springs:

1) <u>Library Center Schedule of Operations:</u> The Contractor shall operate the Library Center (facility at 300 South Sunrise Way) on a twelve (12) month, six (6) day per week, fifty-five (55) hour per week schedule (exclusive of authorized municipal holidays). During this operational schedule all "Public Services" sections (reference, adult circulation, audiovisual, youth services and room rentals) will be available to the public. In addition, Contractor shall provide professional staff for at least seven (7) hours per week when the Library Center is closed to the public (for training, shelving, collection maintenance and meetings) to ensure that the quality of services remains high during the normal operational schedule (55 hours per week). The Contractor may increase the normal operational schedule during the term of this Agreement, but may not decrease it. Any increases in service beyond those described in this Agreement shall be funded by the Contractor, and not the City's General Fund.

2) <u>Acquisitions:</u> The contractor commits to expending at least the following amounts for new acquisitions (circulating and non-circulating books, record-

ings, periodicals and electronic databases) to the Library Center exclusive of cataloging, ordering and processing costs:"

	FY '96–'97	'97–'98	'98–'99	'99–'00	'00–'01
From contract allocation	$142,100	145,000	150,000	150,000	155,000
From supplemental	67,900	70,000	70,000	75,000	75,000
sources	$210,000	$215,000	$220,000	$225,000	$230,000

These amounts shall be employed to acquire at least 7,000 new volumes each fiscal year divided among all public services sections.

3) <u>New Acquisitions "turn around time"</u>: The contractor commits to an average "turn around time" (time from receipt to public availability of new acquisitions) of seven calendar days or less for all new circulating and reference acquisitions.

4) <u>Staffing</u>: Contractor commits to all public services sections of the Library Center having adequate staffing to competently handle the demands for public library services. At least eight (8) full-time equivalent positions will be reserved for "professional" librarians possessing either a Masters Degree in Library Science or more than five years experience as a "professional" public librarian.

5) <u>Automation</u>: Contractor commits to employing current, efficient and "service-oriented" automation equipment in Technical Services, and all public services sections. This includes a fully automated circulation system with 24 hour per day "dial-up" capability. New automation equipment (circulation control, public access cataloging, serials control, electronic cataloging, bibliographic records, patron records and database access) will be acquired within the resources of this Agreement and without seeking additional funding from the City's General Fund. Maintenance of existing and future automation equipment from the Library Department will continue to be funded and supervised via the City's designated manager of such equipment.

6) <u>Historical Museums</u>: Contractor commits to the management and supervision of the Cornelia White House, Palm Springs Historical Society Museum, and the "Ruddy General Store" Museum in conjunction with the Palm Springs Historical Society and museum contractor Mr. Jim Ruddy.

7) <u>Former Crocker Library</u>: The contractor shall continue to manage the existing lease and future uses of the former Crocker branch library (2555 Via Miraleste).

EXHIBIT "B"

COMPENSATION SCHEDULE

The City agrees to allocate funding for management of municipal public library services under the terms of this Agreement the following annual amounts:

*FY 96–'97	'97–'98	'98–'99	'99–'00	'00–'01
$1,583,326	$1,599,152	$1,615,515	$1,631,302	$1,647,615

These amounts will be allocated at the beginning of each fiscal year via the City's extant budget documents and policies. Payments of claims, vouchers, invoices and other incurred expenses shall be via the City's extant practices and in accordance with all current applicable laws.

All donations, fines, fees, state public library subventions and library revenues generated during the term of this Agreement shall be allocated to the Library Trust Fund and/or the Friends of the Palm Springs Library as determined by the Board of Library Trustees.

*Note: These allocations will be automatically adjusted via council actions to amend the City's compensation plan as it relates to library employees. The adjustments would equal amounts determined via such Council action.

Authorization.

The City has authorized distribution of this Offering Circular.

This Offering Circular has been duly executed and delivered by the City Comptroller of the City on behalf of the City.

[Signature forms omitted for printing purposes.]

[Exhibits attached to this Offering Circular
unavailable at time of printing.]

CHICAGO PUBLIC LIBRARY FOUNDATION CONTRIBUTIONS COMMITTED AS ADDITIONAL RATHER THAN ALTERNATIVE SOURCE OF REVENUE FOR CHICAGO PUBLIC LIBRARY.

The Committee on Finance submitted a report recommending that the City Council pass a proposed ordinance transmitted therewith, authorizing the commitment of private funding by the Chicago Public Library Foundation as additional rather than an alternative source of revenue for the Chicago Public Library.

On motion of Alderman Natarus, the said proposed ordinance was *Passed* by yeas and nays as follows:

Yeas—Alderman Roti, Rush, Tillman, T. Evans, Bloom, Robinson, Beavers, Caldwell, Shaw, Vrdolyak, Huels, Fary, Madrzyk, Burke, Langford, Streeter, Kellam, Sheahan, Jones, J. Evans, Garcia, Krystyniak, Henry, Gutierrez, Butler, Smith, Davis, Hagopian, Figueroa, Gabinski, Mell, Austin, Kotlarz, Banks, Cullerton, Pucinski, Natarus, Eisendrath, Hansen, Levar, Shiller, Schulter, Osterman, Orr, Stone—45.

Nays—None.

Alderman Beavers moved to reconsider the foregoing vote. The motion was lost.

The following is said ordinance as passed:

WHEREAS, The Board of Trustees of the Chicago Public Library (the "Board") is charged with the responsibility of supporting and maintaining the Chicago Public Library (the "Library") for the purpose of meeting the research, information, recreation and cultural needs of all residents of the City of Chicago (the "City") by providing them with information in a variety of formats, exhibits, services and programs; and

WHEREAS, The Board has facilitated the organization of the Chicago Public Library Foundation (the "Foundation") for the purpose of soliciting contributions and funding for the Library from individuals, foundations and corporations ("Private Funds" or "Private Funding") in an effort to create a substantial permanent endowment and to provide additional funding for the Library; and

WHEREAS, The Foundation's fundraising efforts are designed to supplement the efforts of the City and the Board to secure from the public and private sectors, monies to fund other ongoing Library activities and acquisitions and related financial needs ("Public Funds" or "Public Funding"); and

WHEREAS, The goal of the Foundation is to raise Private Funds to complement and augment Public Funding in a cooperative effort to support, enrich and enhance the Library; and

WHEREAS, The Library will benefit from the Foundation's cooperative efforts to correspondingly raise Private Funding levels in order to assist the Library in attaining its goals and objectives of quality services; and

WHEREAS, The Library depends on the long-term, continued and increasing commitment of the City, as the bearer of a great public trust, to provide Public Funds for the Library, such Public Funding being enhanced by the philanthropic commitment on the part of individuals, corporations and foundations ("Foundation Contributors") to provide Private Funding for the Library; and

WHEREAS, The success of Foundation efforts to raise Private Funds is contingent upon and facilitated by (i) establishing and maintaining an independent private sector organization such as the Foundation, (ii) private sector donors being assured that their gifts will not be offset by corresponding reductions in Public Funding, and (iii) some form of public acknowledgement of gifts and contributions, as memorialized by a plaque, book plates and the like; and

WHEREAS, As a condition precedent to a $1,000,000 donation from the Pritzker Foundation, pursuant to a grant letter dated March 25, 1987 (the

"Pritzker Letter"), and consistent with the intent of the $1,250,000 donation from the John D. and Catherine T. MacArthur Foundation, it is appropriate and in the best interests of the City that the City demonstrate its commitment that Private Funding provided by the Foundation is to be devoted exclusively to developing and augmenting the resources and services of the Library not otherwise heretofore provided; and

WHEREAS, In order for the Foundation to be successful and effective in its fundraising efforts and to achieve its articulated goals, the City and the State of Illinois (the "State") must commit to be integrally involved throughout the process; now, therefore,

Be It Ordained by the City Council of the City of Chicago:

SECTION 1. Private Funding contributed by the Foundation for the benefit of the Library will be considered as an additional, not an alternative source of revenue for the Library and increased Private Funding will not be the basis or justification for offsetting reductions in Public Funding by the City.

SECTION 2. There should not be included in any ordinance proposed to the City Council, including without limitation any proposed annual appropriation ordinance or any ordinance authorizing the sale of bonds, a recommendation proposing a reduction from amounts which would otherwise be included therein because of Private Funding raised or expected to be raised by the Foundation.

SECTION 3. The City will use its best efforts to cooperate and assist the Foundation in its efforts to solicit Private Funding and to cause the State of Illinois to commit to continued funding and support of the Library.

SECTION 4. The City will cooperate with and assist the Foundation's Staff and Allocations Committee in efforts to develop a specific spending agenda (the "Spending Agenda") for Private Funds. The Private Funds given to the Library will be use-restricted and targeted for programs the Foundation has identified pursuant to the Spending Agenda, within the time frames specified therein.

SECTION 5. This ordinance shall be in full force and effect from and after its passage.

APPROVAL OF DESIGNATED ZONE ORGANIZATIONS FOR ENTERPRISE ZONES I, II AND IV.

The Committee on Finance submitted a report recommending that the City Council pass four proposed ordinances transmitted therewith, designating certain organizations as "Designated Zone Organizations" for City of Chicago Enterprise Zones I, II and IV.

On motion of Alderman Natarus, the said proposed ordinances were *Passed* by yeas and nays as follows:

Yeas—Alderman Roti, Rush, Tillman, T. Evans, Bloom, Robinson, Beavers, Caldwell, Shaw, Vrdolyak, Huels, Fary, Madrzyk, Burke, Langford, Streeter, Kellam, Sheahan, Jones, J. Evans, Garcia, Krystyniak, Henry, Gutierrez, Butler, Smith, Davis, Hagopian, Figueroa, Gabinski, Mell, Austin, Kotlarz, Banks, Cullerton, Pucinski, Natarus, Eisendrath, Hansen, Levar, Shiller, Schulter, Osterman, Orr, Stone—45.

Nays—None.

Alderman Beavers moved to reconsider the foregoing vote. The motion was lost.

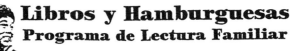

Libros y Hamburguesas
Programa de Lectura Familiar

¡Proximamente Aquí!

Adonde: Escuela Elemental Pueblo Gardens
              2210 E. Calle 33

Cuando: Cada segunda y cuarto martes del mes
              a las 6:15 p.m. - 8:15 p.m.

¡MARQUE SU CALENDARIO!
Primera sesión: martes, 23 de enero a las 6:15

Traiga a toda su familia . . .

¡Disfrute de la lectura en familia y además programas especiales!

Cada miembro de familia que asiste puede gozar de la cena (Big Mac, papitas, y bebida). Debe apuntarse a 6:25 p.m. para recibir su comida gratis de McDonald's.

- ♥ 6:15 p.m. a 7:15 p.m. – libros
- ♥ 7:15 p.m. a 8:15 p.m. – hamburguesas

Ayuda a sus hijos a empezar bien en la escuela y en la vida . . .

- ♥ Registre a su familia y recibirán sus tarjetas para la Biblioteca.
- ♥ Lea con sus niños durante el programa y por toda la semana.
- ♥ Durante la semana apunte el tiempo que lee con sus niños.
- ♥ Ayude y supervise a sus niños en "Libros y Hamburguesas."

¡¡Porque los niños que LEEN pueden hacerlo todo!!

Patrocinados por PIMA YOUTH PARTNERSHIP * TUCSON-PIMA PUBLIC LIBRARY * PUEBLO GARDENS ELEMENTARY SCHOOL * MCDONALD'S

Para más información, llame a la Escuela Elemental Pueblo Gardens
617-6300

'The Procurement System in the Government is Like a Jigsaw Puzzle.'

–Helen Dennis, The Project Advantage Group

The Project Advantage Group, 5555 Airport Highway, Toledo, continually seeks new business by bidding on government contracts.

Helen Dennis, president, explains:

"The procurement system in government is like a jigsaw puzzle, with lots of pieces. Success is only possible when you can put all the pieces together. The Library's Government Procurement Center (GPC) helps you do that.

"Specifically, the GPC helps me understand the system (including forms, codes, regulations, rules, policies, etc.), contact people in government agencies, research and review proposals.

"I think the GPC is a major contributor to the economic development of our community.

"The **Library's Business Department**, as a whole, has a wealth of information and resources. As a small business, I don't have an extensive resource/research department – the Library plays that role for me."

The Project Advantage Group provides consultative and management services to major corporations, organizations and government agencies that are undergoing major relocation and facility projects. The focus is to help organize such efforts, maintain operations with a minimum of disruption, and assure the project gets done on time and within budget.

Toledo-Lucas County Public Library
Your Source.

WHAT'S SO GREAT ABOUT THE BROOKLYN PUBLIC LIBRARY?

IT'S BIG!

Books. Magazines. Newspapers. Pamphlets. Videos. Audiocassettes. CDs. Books-on-tape. Sheet music. And of course, computers. The Brooklyn Public Library has information nearly in every form within its 6.1 million-strong holdings. Our Business Library has the largest such collection in the nation.

Wherever you live, the library is there. Our Central Library, Business Library, 58 branches and Bookmobile, with their broad range of services and programs, make us an integral part of every Brooklyn neighborhood. With more than 1.4 million borrowers, it's hard to know every one — but we're striving to fill the needs of each person who looks to us for information, education and inspiration.

IT'S ENLIGHTENING

Parlez-vous français — or want to? You'll find books in 64 languages in the Central Library alone.

Need to check a fact? Telephone our reference service at the Central Library or Business Library. Last year alone, we answered inquiries from more than 133,000 callers.

Thinking of taking a few courses, or of changing jobs? Our Education and Job Information Center offers national job postings, resume help, and a wide assortment of directories and catalogs.

Whether you're a "regular," or simply wish you could visit more often ... looking for a "how-to" video, or the latest best seller, the library puts the world at your fingertips.

IT'S AGELESS

From preschoolers to senior citizens — and everyone in between — the Brooklyn Public Library has something for everyone.

For the younger set, there are story hours and, at 11 locations, The Child's Place — a special place where preschoolers get a solid start on a lifetime of learning.

Older kids find a full range of after-school activities at the Library, along with *Reading Is Fundamental* — an incentive program that encourages youngsters to read, and places books in homes that otherwise might not be able to afford them.

Lectures, book discussion groups and

a whole series of events for older adults, including health fairs and exercise programs, make our libraries neighborhood centers of learning and activity.

IT'S ENTERTAINING

Puppet shows at the Library? Concerts? Movies? Art exhibits?

Yes, and that's only the beginning. The Library is much more than books on shelves. It is a place where all of the arts flourish — from retrospectives of established authors ... to celebrations of Brooklyn-born artists ... to dramas by bold, new voices. Check out our monthly Calendar of Events, and join us soon!

IT'S OUTGOING

"Service" is an often-used word in our vocabulary — a mission that extends the Library's reach far beyond its walls.

Our Bookmobile, with its 3,000 books is our most visible emissary. We also keep a window on the world open for the homebound — elderly neighbors who live in nursing homes, hospitals and senior residences — by delivering books right to them.

Appallingly, one in five adult New Yorkers cannot read or write well enough to decipher simple directions or fill out a job application. For those Brooklynites motivated to improve themselves, our adult Literacy Program offers free tutoring and computer-assisted instruction.

The Patriot-News

MONDAY, MAY 12, 1997 • PAGE A8

A Free Press — Armor of the Republic

RAYMOND L. GOVER
PUBLISHER

EDWIN F. RUSSELL
PRESIDENT

CAROLINE D. HARRISON
GENERAL MANAGER

JOHN A. KIRKPATRICK
EDITOR

DALE A. DAVENPORT
EDITORIAL PAGE EDITOR

THOMAS B. BADEN JR.
MANAGING EDITOR

HARRISBURG, PENNSYLVANIA

'YES' ON LIBRARIES

Perry Countians should resist notion that this referendum is about 'taxes'

You don't find many people who are against libraries. Even people who don't know which end of a book is up instinctively know that you don't bad-mouth libraries. That would be like coming out against apple pie and mother.

But up in Perry County, which will vote on implementing a half-mill library tax on May 20, some folks have found a way to dislike libraries without saying so. They say something to the effect: "The libraries are great. I just can't afford to pay another dollar of taxes or I'm going to lose my home."

Love libraries, hate taxes.

Well, here's a news flash for all those of that persuasion: The free public library isn't free. Books cost money. Buildings cost money. Insurance costs money. Librarians cost money.

In fact, it is rather amazing that Perry County has any libraries at all, inasmuch as it ranks dead last among Pennsylvania's 67 counties in local government support for libraries. Last year, county commissioners provided all of $10,000 toward the support of Perry's four libraries. This year it provided nothing.

So it isn't as if the taxpayers of Perry County have been ravaged in support of libraries. Neighboring Juniata County, with half the population, seems by comparison an oasis of cultural enlightenment. County government this year appropriated $80,500 to its single library.

The library tax to be voted on would amount to $5.55 for the average Perry County homeowner, hardly enough to order a pizza. And somebody's going to lose their home because of this imposition? The elderly will be made to suffer as a result? Do the opponents and complainers who have made such statements have an ounce of credibility?

The danger here — and it is a real one — is that the library tax referendum will be seen by many as it is being portrayed by its opponents — as a referendum on property taxes. If you don't like taxes, vote "No."

If that's the intended message, it's not one that is going to survive translation. In fact, a "No" plurality will be seen for what it is, a vote against libraries, a vote for ignorance. Indeed, such an outcome would have the ironic impact of proving how desperately the libraries need to expand their reach in Perry County.

This is not the place to take a stand against property taxation, the reform of which this newspaper has long championed.

Rather, we would urge the voters of Perry County to reject the naysayers and cast their ballots in support of the proposition that libraries enrich our lives and communities, and are more than worth their modest cost.

THE LIBRARY

April 1997

Including 1997/98 budget vote information

ENRICHING RECIPE

for Wondrous Library Fare

INGREDIENTS

- choice books
- a bunch of rare local history resources
- potpourri of periodicals
- variety of videos
- young adult selections
- children's programs
- top-notch technology
- dedicated staff
- buildings that will serve well into the 21st century

DIRECTIONS

MIX in the first 5 ingredients.

SIFT in selections from special collections.

WHIP in some top-notch technology at PC and Internet Stations.

SPICE with compact disc reference resources and online databases.

WHISK in young adult paperbacks, audiobooks, and homework center features.

FROST with storytimes and Preschoolers' Door to Learning programs.

BLEND with a friendly and dedicated staff.

SERVE in buildings that will satisfy the information and entertainment appetites of library patrons well into the 21st century.

Bon Appetit!

SAVE PASADENA'S LIBRARY

Dear Neighbor,

    I'm not the kind of person to get up on a soapbox, but this is important.

    Our library's in trouble. And I'm writing to you because without your help, very soon we won't have much library left.

    No, this letter isn't to ask you for money. Or have you write letters. Or march in protest down Colorado Boulevard.

    I'm writing to ask you to use the most powerful weapon you have to save Pasadena's library, <u>Your vote.</u>

    And I've even enclosed a form you can use to make it possible to vote from your home.

    You see, we're facing an emergency. <u>Our library is being financially choked to death.</u>

    Here's what's happening. Over the last few years the state budget crisis has forced Pasadena to make huge cuts in city services. And where have many of those cuts been made? The library.

-- <u>One third of central library hours have been eliminated in the last year. It's already closed on Mondays, and Sundays will go next.</u>

-- <u>Branch libraries are closed three days a week.</u> <u>Some face permanent closure.</u>

-- <u>The budget to buy books has been slashed by two thirds.</u> <u>And worn or damaged books are no longer being repaired.</u>

-- <u>Vital services like reference, children's hours and literacy programs are disappearing.</u>

-- <u>Over 300 newspaper and magazine subscriptions have been canceled.</u>

-- <u>Staff training has been completely eliminated.</u>

    If nothing is done to stop it, Pasadena's once proud public library will soon be just a memory.

    <u>That's why it's so important for us to pass the library funding measure on the special election, June 22nd.</u>

    This measure will restore lost services, prevent further cuts and protect the library from losing out in a political tug-of-war: The library will no longer have to compete with the police and fire departments for its fair share of funds.

                                            (over, please)

87 North Raymond Avenue, Suite 315 ✛ Pasadena, CA 91103 ✛ (818) 793-8050

The measure authorizes a special tax of just $20 a year for each homeowner in Pasadena. That's just a nickel a day. Businesses and landlords would pay slightly more. And every penny goes to the library.

People with low incomes, houses of worship and community service organizations would be exempt. And in five years the tax will expire unless the voters decide to renew it.

It's a solution that's fair, effective, and affordable.

But the measure requires two thirds of the voters to say "yes." Even one person less than two thirds and it won't pass.

That's why I'm urging you to vote YES for our library on election day. You could be the one person who makes the difference.

And to make it easy, I've enclosed a form for you to request an absentee ballot from City Hall. If you have not already requested an absentee ballot, all you have to do is sign this form and mail it back in the postage-paid envelope I've provided. Or, you can use the request form attached to the sample ballot sent to you by the City.

Either way, you'll receive your absentee ballot by return mail and you'll be able to vote by mail without making a trip to the polls.

By passing this special measure we can save the legacy previous generations have left us and reverse the destruction of our library.

-- Central library will reopen in the mornings and on Mondays.

-- Branch libraries will be open five days a week.

-- The budget for books and periodicals will be restored.

-- Vital programs for children and the disadvantaged will be resumed.

In the end, the kind of city we live in -- the kind of world we live in -- is up to us. And the choices we make about what's important, and what has value, is how our world gets shaped.

Maybe it's just the way I was brought up, but it seems to me that the library has to be one of those things that's important. And if we don't think of it as a treasure worth protecting, what does that say about our city? About what we want for our children and grandchildren?

Please vote "yes" to save Pasadena's library. Thanks.

Sincerely,

Orel Hershiser

Orel Hershiser

P.S. I said I wasn't going to ask for money, and I'm not. But just in case you'd like to help cover some of the cost of the campaign to pass this ballot measure, there's a space on the reply form for you to indicate that. (No city or library money goes into this campaign; it all comes from people like you and me who care about our library.)

739 MAIN STREET, HARWICH, MA 02645 △ (508) 430-7562

LOOK AT BROOKS

FACTS ABOUT THE BROOKS LIBRARY BUILDING PROJECT
Published by The Friends of Brooks Free Library - Fall, 1995

WHAT DOES THE LIBRARY BUILDING NEED?

The existing building needs repairs to its structure, fire protection, plumbing & heating systems. The interior needs to be de-leaded and painted. The building needs to be insulated and there are additional safety issues that need to be addressed.

The facilities are inadequate to meet the current needs of the existing population. It is simply too small.

The building is not in compliance with the Americans with Disabilities Act (ADA) laws. At least 12% of the residents of Harwich consider themselves disabled, according to the 1990 census.

WHAT IS THE HISTORY OF THE PROJECT?
The Brooks Free Library has been a center for information, education and enjoyment to Harwich for more than 100 years. Its services and resources are free to all residents of the town. The building is listed in the National Historic Register and is a recognized landmark. It was last repaired in 1972.

1990 - The Trustees of the Library, working closely with the Town Engineer, library consultant and appropriate Town and State Committees, started to examine existing problems and review potential solutions.

1991 - A survey of Harwich residents showed overwhelming support for preserving the Library as a valued, historic piece of architecture and an important part of Harwich's heritage. In addition, the survey showed a strong interest in adult education programs, discussion groups, reference materials and media. The rear entrance & parking lot were especially cited as problems. There was moderate support for additional staff.

1992 - A study and assessment of needs continued and a long-range strategic plan was adopted and distributed. The Building Program was written and discussed at public meeting. The Designer Selection Committee was appointed.

1993 - Architectural firms submitted proposals and were interviewed. The firm of Childs, Bertman, Tseckares was selected. Designs were discussed in open meetings. The Building Committee was appointed.

1994 - A unanimous vote at Town Meeting allowed the expenditure of funds for architectural plans of renovation and addition. This expenditure was approved in the ballot override.

1995 - Voters approved the submission of plans in an attempt to get State funds. The first-round grant application received high ratings, but failed, primarily because of parking problems and inadequate staffing issues. Maintenance costs continue to be researched. The Friends of Brooks Library are purchasing an adjacent lot with the express purpose of resolving parking problems. A second-round grant application is under review and will be submitted. The Building Committee is exploring ways to reduce costs in order to finalize exact construction specifications and bids.

1996 - Residents will vote on funding this project at Town Meeting.

PLEASE TURN OVER

LOOK ʌT BROOKS (CONTINUED)

WHY DID BUDGET AMOUNTS CHANGE?

The legal, municipal processes required of a project of this kind are complex and binding. As with any project, costs become more clearly defined as the facts and considerations are determined. In addition, inflation is always a factor. Throughout the process, cost estimates were discussed and acknowledged to be imprecise and premature, however, they sometimes appeared in the press as actual costs.

WHY WERE THESE PLANS CHOSEN?

The chosen plans have been carefully reviewed. They adhere to stated objectives, address future needs of a growing community and are architecturally pleasing and economically sound and efficient. They make sense.

WHY WAS THE FIRST ROUND OF THE STATE GRANT WITHHELD?

The application round was extremely competitive. 71 communities submitted proposals - 28 were approved for some sort of funding. In their review of the Brooks Library plans, The Massachusetts Board of Library Commissioners said "the planning process and Building Program are rated excellent.... the exterior design is outstanding and even exciting... this design is appropriate and compelling." The weaknesses concerned inadequate parking and understaffing.

WHAT ARE THE CHOICES?

Do the necessary repairs and bring the present building up to code.
Consequences: Costs are estimated at one million dollars; the Library's present usable space decreases by one third and future needs are ignored. These costs do not include the substantial expenditures already made for plans that would not be used.

Proceed with the renovation/addition plans.
Consequences: Costs are estimated at three million dollars, with final construction bids due in Spring of 1996. Because of retiring debts, this is an optimum time for the Town to fund such a project. The Library expansion is in accordance with the Capital Plan. In addition, the Brooks Free Library would retain its historic and architectural integrity and value. As the "cornerstone" of Harwich Center, it would continue to be an integral part of the revitalization of the area. The Library would expand its services, add additional computer resources and be accessible to everyone. The plans are designed to meet the needs of the community for 20 years.

LOOK ʌT BROOKS

RESIDENTS WILL VOTE ON FUNDING THIS PROJECT AT TOWN MEETING IN 1996

ON-GOING RELATIONS WITH PUBLIC OFFICIALS

It is important to establish a regular, year-round working relationship with public officials and their staff. Not only do we need to ask them for their assistance in securing additional resources, but it is vital to notify them regularly of programs and activities in the branches. Sending program flyers and other materials to legislators' offices will demonstrate to them the diversity of services available in the library. For your use, it is recommended that you keep an informational folder on your local elected representatives consisting of current daily and local newspaper articles, campaign materials, and legislative mailings.

Branch Librarians do the following to maintain a working relationship with members of the City Council, the State Legislature, Members of Congress, and their staffs:

- send program flyers, branch announcements, support group meeting announcements or other material to district offices on a regular basis, perhaps with a card or handwritten note;
- invite public officials to visit the branch;
- visit district offices.

VISITS BY PUBLIC OFFICIALS TO THE BRANCHES

There is no substitute for public officials experiencing firsthand the variety of services the Library provides. Regional and Branch Librarians, in consultation with the Borough Office and Government Affairs Office, periodically extend invitations to public officials.

Branch Librarians do the following when preparing for a visit by a public official:

- choose a day and time when the branch is the busiest or is having special activities or programs;
- invite support people and ask them to serve as co-hosts;
- consider inviting representatives of the Community Board or other local organizations;
- consider arranging local news coverage of the visit;
- tell public officials—either by mail or telephone—the full details of the visit: the agenda, how long they should plan to stay, who they will be speaking to and for how long, how many people will be present, and give them directions to the branch;
- follow-up a written invitation with a telephone call to confirm;
- call the legislator's office the day before the visit to reconfirm;
- brief the elected official on the Library's expense and capital needs, and the characteristics of the branch and its users;

- arrange for local press coverage; and
- coordinate all activities with Government Affairs Office.

On the day of the visit, assign one person to the front door to serve as a greeter. Be prepared to display a full range of library services within the time frame of your guest's visit. Give the public official a written statement of funding requests, and an assortment of library literature. Always remember to thank the public official for visiting, and for his or her support of libraries. Send a thank-you note to supporters who participated in the visit.

INFORMATIONAL VISITS TO ELECTED OFFICIALS' OFFICES

Sometimes a visit by Library supporters or staff to an elected official's office is more convenient or appropriate than a visit to a branch. A visit to an elected official's office may allow for more thorough discussion of specific targeted issues. There is a disadvantage of this approach, however: the public official misses the opportunity to see first hand, the diversity of services provided by the library, and see users in the branch.

Remember to ask the elected official to take very specific actions on behalf of libraries. Asking them for support is not enough. For example, ask public officials to:

(1) talk to their leadership and urge them to support increased library funding and;

(2) urge their colleagues to talk to leadership about increased funding.

Regional Librarians and Branch Librarians should coordinate visits in consultation with the Borough Office and Government Affairs Office. When arranging a meeting with a public official either by library staff or supporters:

- consult with other Branch Librarians in the district to see if they or their supporters would like to attend;
- arrange for a manageable group of three or four visitors;
- make a definite appointment and send a confirmation letter;
- provide everybody attending the visit with the information they need concerning the time, date, place and travel time, and brief them on the issues to be discussed;
- remember that time will be limited, so there should only be one or two main points of discussion;
- plan for a three-minute presentation, including discussion;
- have your group meet before the meeting to review the issues and main points and to discuss strategy;
- take pertinent position papers, fact sheets, Library literature and business cards to distribute;
- reconfirm the appointment before you go;
- hand your card to the aide upon arrival, and ask to see the legislator;
- ask to speak to an aide if the legislator is unable to keep the appointment;
- designate one person to take the lead and introduce the group, one person to take notes, and one person to direct discussion back to the library issues should discussion wander away from the main points;
- try to establish a friendly atmosphere;
- keep your presentation direct and concise;

- be specific in what you request from the elected official;
- send a short thank-you letter restating the main points, answering questions that arose, and reminding the elected official of what he or she promised to do;
- send a thank-you note to all those supporters that participated;
- coordinate all activities with Government Affairs Office; and
- send Government Affairs Office an update on visit.

NEWSLETTER

Volume V,   Number III

DECEMBER 1996

EXPANSION BUDGET PASSES!

On October 15, 1996, the residents of the Greenport and Oysterponds School Districts voted overwhelmingly for the expansion and renovation of the Floyd Memorial Library. Congratulations everyone!

Voting day was very exciting as more than five hundred people in the two school districts came out to express their interest in the future of library service at Floyd Memorial Library.

The architect has begun the process of obtaining a building permit from the Village of Greenport, meeting the various boards and presenting our plans for their approval. Once the building permit has been obtained, the final design stage will proceed. Early next year the final working drawings and bid documents will be completed. After bids are invited, reviewed, and awarded, a ground breaking ceremony will be held in late spring.

NEW BUILDING GIFT OPPORTUNITIES

During the public hearings leading up to the successful expansion referendum, the Board of Trustees affirmed its intention to seek both public grants and private gifts to help finance the expansion/renovation project. Two funds have already been established in memory of Frank Giorgi and Russ Terry, longtime faithful Library Board members and volunteers.

Other residents and friends are encouraged to consider gifts, memorials, or bequests at this time. Either Donald VanCleef, President of the Library Board or Lisa Richland, the Library Director will be pleased to talk with you about opportunities for large or small gifts and possible memorial designations.

Floyd Memorial Library

SAVE PUBLIC LIBRARIES

The County's Office of Management and Budget has asked the Prince George's County Memorial Library System to submit a budget for fiscal year 1998 in the amount of $13,886,916, a figure that is $1.6 million below this year's budget of $15,486,916. This is a reduction of 10.33%. The Library cannot count on receiving a $2 million supplemental budget from the Governor as it has in the past.

What does this mean for the Library System and your neighborhood library?

*It could mean the elimination of 38 fulltime positions—librarians, circulation assistants, drivers, maintenance workers and clerks

*It could end library services on Sundays at the Laurel, Surratts-Clinton, and New Carrollton libraries

*It could reduce the budget for purchase of books, CD's, videos and magazines by over $300,000

*It could mean a reduction in utility and maintenance services

*It could mean that ALL libraries would be open fewer hours each week

The Library administration, Board of Trustees, and Friends of Prince George's County Libraries will do everything they can to close this budget gap. BUT, whether this proposed budget and the drastic cuts become a reality, or our elected officials restore the full budget, depends on you.

What can you do?

*Join your local Friends of the Library organization

*Write to your County Council Member and the County Executive. Tell them why the Library is important to you and your family. Tell them why it is important to education, business and the life of the community. Protest this reduction in the Library's budget and let the County know that you expect full funding for the Library.

Prepared by the Friends of the Prince George's County Libraries. [Jan. 1997]

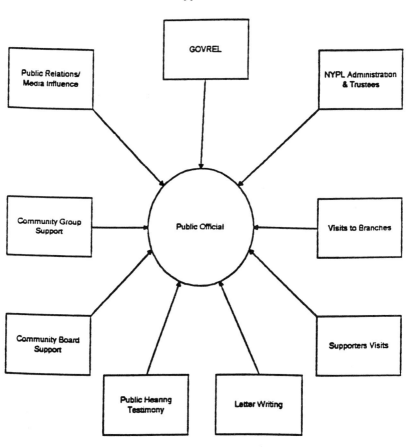

In FY 1994, 82 percent of funding for the Branch Libraries was provided by the City of New York, nine percent from the State of New York, and one percent from the Federal government. The Branch Libraries also received funding, amounting to four percent of the budget, from private donors for certain special projects, and another four percent came from "other revenue."

THE NEW YORK PUBLIC LIBRARY

OFFICE OF GOVERNMENTAL AFFAIRS AND PROGRAMS

STATEMENT OF NEW YORK CITY FY 1995 EXPENSE PRIORITIES

- Annualization of 6-days of service in The Branch Libraries and The Research Libraries.

- An increase in funding for books and materials to continue to re-build the collections in the branches.

- Funding to restore additional hours in the units of the Central Branch Libraries, which include the Mid-Manhattan Library, the Library for the Performing Arts at Lincoln Center and the Donnell Library Center.

- Additional funding for staff and materials for the New York City Collections in The Research Libraries.

- Funding to begin systemwide phase-in of the Connecting Libraries and Schools Project (CLASP).

- Increased funding for literacy, including Adult Basic Education (ABE), family literacy and English as a Second Language (ESL) programs.

- Funding for staff to adequately serve and respond to those in most critical need of library service: children, teens, older adults, the business community, new immigrants, job seekers, the disabled and other prime users.

September 14, 1993

Drop Everything and Write!

During Drop Everything and Read Week, April 12 - 19, New Yorkers Read More Books than Ever Before!

THANK MAYOR GIULIANI AND THE CITY COUNCIL FOR MAINTAINING SIX DAYS OF SERVICE AND PLEASE ASK FOR INCREASED FUNDING FOR:

- **Books and Materials**
- **Connecting Libraries and Schools Project (CLASP)**
- **Restoration of Sunday Service at the Borough Centers**
- **Restoration of Literacy Classes**
- **60 Hour Weeks at Mid-Manhattan**
- **Research Libraries' Services**

The New York Public Library

50 East Huron Street
Chicago, Illinois 60611-2795
USA

Telephone 312 944 6780
Fax 312 440 9374
Toll Free 800 545 2433
TDD 312 944 7298
E-mail: ala@ala.org
http://www.ala.org

ALAAmericanLibraryAssociation

Contact: Public Information Office
312-280-5042/5043

Log-on . . .

Check out the latest information about ALA public awareness and advocacy programs on the ALA Web page at http://www.ala.org

Look under **Events** for updates on National Library Week, Library Card Sign-Up month and other library promotional events. Sample press materials, art work and other helpful information are provided.

ALA News Releases can be found on the ALA homepage under News & Views.

Sign on to electronic discussion lists:

- *PR Talk* – Idea-sharing and updates on ALA promotional activities and library PR issues. (list name: prtalk)

- *Library Advocacy Now!* -- Idea-sharing, updates and legislative alerts of special interest to library advocates. (list name: aladnow)

- *ALA News Releases* – Receive ALA news releases online. (list name: alanews)

To subscribe, send message to: listproc@ala.org. Leave the subject line blank. In the body of the message, type: subscribe (name of list) (your first and last name)

E-mail addresses:
Public Information Office – pio@ala.org (General inquiries/materials requests)
Linda Wallace, Director, Public Information Office – lwallace@ala.org
Deborah Davis, PR Specialist – dedavis@ala.org
Joyce Kelly, Press Officer – jkelly@ala.org
Belia Ortega, PR Assistant – bortega@ala.org

References and Related Sources

American Library Association. "Equity on the Information Superhighway." *LibraryAd-vocacyNow!* (action pack). Chicago: ALA, 1995 (and subsequent editions).

———. *Libraries Online!* Chicago: ALA, 1997.

American Library Directory, 1997–1998. 50th ed. New York: Bowker, 1997.

Anderson, Albert. *Ethics for Fundraisers.* Bloomington: Indiana University Press, 1996.

Andreason, Alan R. "Profits for Nonprofits: Find a Corporate Partner." *Harvard Business Review,* November-December 1996.

Bailey, Anne Lowrey. "How a New Idea Saved the San Francisco Library's Stalled Capital Campaign." *The Chronicle of Philanthropy,* July 12, 1994, p. 27.

Baltimore County Public Library's Blue Ribbon Committee. *Give 'Em What They Want! Managing the Public's Library.* Chicago: ALA, 1992.

Beckerman, Edwin. *Politics and the American Public Library: Creating Political Support for Library Goals.* Lanham, Md.: Scarecrow Press, 1996.

Berry, John. "Broward County Library, Library of the Year." *Library Journal,* June 15, 1996.

———. "The Central Library—Beyond Symbolism: Our Mission Is More Than Slaking Popular Thirst" (editorial). *Library Journal,* June 1, 1990.

———. "The Problem Is Political" (editorial). *Library Journal,* April 15, 1997.

———. "'Vision' Is Not Enough" (editorial). *Library Journal,* February 15, 1997.

Burlingame, Dwight F. *Library Fundraising: Models for Success.* Chicago: ALA, 1995.

California Library Association et al. "Restructuring California Public Libraries." *Joint Task Force Report.* Executive summary, 1995.

Craft, M. A. "Private Funds versus Public Funds—the Ball Is in the Library's Court." *The Bottom Line,* vol. 8, no. 4 (1995), pp. 5–9.

Crawford, Walt, and Michael Gorman. *Future Libraries: Dreams, Madness and Reality.* Chicago: ALA, 1995.

Croneberger, Robert B. "External Influences on Public Library Management in the 21st Century." *Journal of Library Administration* (1989), pp. 209–20.

Crowley, Bill. "Library Lobbying as a Way of Life." *Public Libraries,* March/April 1994, pp. 96–98.

Dolnick, Sandy, ed. *Friends of Libraries Sourcebook.* 2nd ed. Philadelphia: FOLUSA, 1990.

Fisher, Roger, William Ury, and Bruce Patton. *Getting to Yes.* 2nd ed. New York: Penguin, 1991.

Gaul, Gilbert M. "Libraries in Distress." *Philadelphia Inquirer* online. 4 parts, June 1–4, 1997. http://www.phillynews.com/packages/libraries.

Glennon, Michael L. "Developing and Passing a Bond Issue." *Public Libraries,* January/February 1997, pp. 24–28.

Hall, Richard B. *Winning Library Referenda Campaigns: A How-to-Do-It Manual, #50.* New York: Neal-Schuman, 1995.

Holt, Gordy. "My Turn, Says the Seattle Library." *Seattle Post Intelligencer,* March 17, 1997.

Hoover, James W., and Heather Dale. *Hoosier Art Collection of the Kokomo-Howard County Public Library* (Kokomo, Ind.: The Library, 1989).

Hubbard, Elizabeth Ryan. "A Conflict of Values: An Inquiry into the Impact of Local Political Decision-Making on the Funding of the Carnegie Library of Pittsburgh in Three Selected Decades." Ph.D. diss., University of Pittsburgh, 1996.

Jeavons, Thomas H. *Public Libraries and Private Fundraising: Opportunities and Issues.* Evanston, Ill.: Urban Libraries Council, 1994.

Kehrer, Barbara H. "Seven Reasons to Evaluate." *Foundation News,* January/February 1993.

Kniffel, Leonard. "Criticism Follows Hoopla at New San Francisco Library." *American Libraries,* August 1996, pp. 12–13.

Kretzmann, John P., and John L. McKnight. *Building Communities from the Inside Out: A Path toward Finding and Mobilizing a Community's Assets.* Chicago: ACTA Publications, 1993.

Libraries for the Future. *Library Advocacy Power Tools.* 2nd ed. New York: Libraries for the Future, 1994.

———. Pub-Adv listserv, 1995–97.

"Library of the Future," Special report in *Datebook, San Francisco Chronicle,* April 7, 1996.

Library Planning Associates, Inc. "A Plan for Library Service in Allegheny County." Draft, Madison, Wis., 1996.

Lucchino, Frank J. "A Quiet Crisis: Libraries in Allegheny County." Special report, Allegheny County Controller's Office, Pittsburgh, Pa., 1991.

Maddox, Robert R. *Team Building: An Exercise in Leadership.* Menlo Park, Calif.: Crisp Publications, 1995.

National Center for Education Statistics. *Public Libraries in the United States: 1993.* Washington, D.C.: Bureau of the Census, September 1995.

New York City Council. "The Transcript of the Minutes of the Preliminary Budget Hearing." Committee on Finance. March 12, 1997, p. 8.

New York Public Library. *Budget Action Handbook.* In-house unpublished document, 1993.

Public Library Association. Public Library Data Service. *Statistical Report '97.* Chicago: ALA, 1997.

Reynolds, Brian A. "Public Library Funding: Issues, Trends and Resources." *Advances in Librarianship,* vol. 18 (1994), pp. 159–88.

Rosso, Henry A., and Associates. *Achieving Excellence in Fund Raising.* San Francisco: Jossey-Bass, 1991.

Rybczynski, Witold. "A Good Public Building [the Chicago Public Library]." *The Atlantic,* vol. 270, no. 2, August 1992.

San Francisco Public Library Foundation. *The New Main* (summer 1991).

Scott, Cynthia D., and Dennis T. Jaffre. *Managing Change at Work.* Rev. ed. Menlo Park, Calif.: Crisp Publications, 1995.

Sherman, Steve. *ABC's of Library Promotion.* 3rd ed. Metuchen, N.J.: Scarecrow Press, 1992.

Steele, Victoria, and Stephen D. Elder. *Becoming a Fundraiser.* Chicago: ALA, 1992.

Swann, James. *Fundraising for the Small Public Library.* New York: Neal-Schuman, 1990.

Thomas, Paulette. "Ohio Nurtures Home-Grown Companies." *Wall Street Journal,* March 31, 1997, p. A2.

Trezza, Alphonse F., ed. *Commitment to Service: The Library's Mission.* Boston: G.K. Hall, 1990.

Turock, Betty J. "Improving Accountability." *The Bottom Line,* vol. 3, no. 4 (1990).

University of California, Berkeley. Pub-Lib listserv, 1996–1997.

Welling, Penny H. "Introducing the Internet in a Rural Setting." *North Carolina Libraries,* winter 1996, pp. 165–68.

Wiegand, Steve, and Nancy Vogel. "A Stack of Troubles: Once-Proud State Libraries Battling Decay." *Sacramento Bee,* September 25, 1994, p. A1.

Young, Sally, and Geni Sowell. "Special Library Tax?" *The Bottom Line,* vol. 7, no. 2 (1993), pp. 8–11.

Index

About the Author

Mary Anne Craft (craftlib@aol.com) is president of Craft Enterprises, Ltd.; a library Friend; and a card-holding user of the Carnegie Library of Pittsburgh and the New York Public Library. She has an A.B. from Wellesley College and an M.L.S. from the University of California, Berkeley.

·